Robert S. King

SELECTED POEMS

FUTURECYCLE PRESS
www.futurecycle.org

Cover artwork, a finessed image of the Laniakea supercluster by Diane Kistner; cover and interior design by Diane Kistner; Gentium Book Basic text and Cronos Pro titling

Library of Congress Control Number: 2023944491

Copyright © 2023 Robert S. King
All Rights Reserved

Published by FutureCycle Press
Athens, Georgia, USA

ISBN 978-1-952593-66-6

Contents

Foreword..7

from
THE HUNTED RIVER

The Juggler Tells His Children of Dreams......................................10
Ice-Sparkles...11
Prophets Climbing to Machu Picchu..12
Fading Pictures..13
The New World Dictionary..14
Going Through the Motions..15
The Meaning of Dogs..16
What Missing the Cat Means..17
The Light Sedative of Dark..18
The Glass Heart...19
Veterans Know a Purr Is Just an Infant Growl...............................20
Confessions of the Slower Sprinter...21
Mirror at the Speed of Light..22
Men..23
The Gentleman Who Woke Up as a Goat..24
Sanctuary...25
Rock Road..26
Motions...27
Regret..28
Road Steam..29
Daydreaming at Rush Hour...30
Ice Steeples, Road Signs..31
Progress..32
River Pulse...33
Lighthouse...34
Cottonmouth Catchers in a Night Swamp......................................35
Dream of the Electric Eel...36
Knots..37
The Hunted River...38
The Treasure of Bone..41
The Wind Is Often Sudden Here..42
The Last Saint of the Empire..43
How Trees Travel...44

from
THE GRAVEDIGGER'S ROOTS

The Gravedigger Pacing His Cage...46
The Gravedigger's Black Apple Beating..47
Burying a Mute...48
Why the Dead Are so Passive...49
Snowhaunt...50
The Ghost Observes His Body..51
The Ghost in the Barn Light..52
Blame It on Genealogy...53

Discoveries of the Shovel...54
Condensation..55
The Gravedigger's Workday...56
Orphans Adopting Themselves..57
Moving to the City..58
The Gravedigger's Plot..59
The Gravedigger Blows on the Bottle..60
The Gravedigger's Night Out...61
The Old Deeds of the Gravedigger...62
The Death of Magic..63
The Gratitude of the Dead..64
Darkness Too Is a Mirror..65
The Gravedigger's Legacy..66
The Graveyard Shift...67
Dream of the Hollow Bone...68
Communion..69
Against the Graveyard's Greater Wall...70
The Gravedigger's Pay Dirt..71
Why Graveyards Are Full of Bright Birds..72
A Wingbeat of Hope...73
Feeding the Body of Earth..74

**from
ONE MAN'S PROFIT**

The Landowners of Pompeii...76
The Flight..77
The Language of Trees...78
Passings...79
Grandmother..80
Homestead..81
On Mother's Day...82
Heart Attack...83
The Dreamer Returns Home...84
After the War, the War..85
Fairy Tale..86
End of the Line..87
One Man's Profit...88
Strategy for Longevity...89
The Bottom...90
Cleaning Up..91
Everlasting Life...92

**from
DIARY OF THE LAST PERSON ON EARTH**

The Last Person on Earth Begins His Diary......................................94
The Last Person on Earth Remembers the Sickness.........................95
The Last Person on Earth Recalls the Looter....................................96
The Last Person on Earth in a Traffic Jam...97
The Last Person on Earth Checks His Email......................................98
The Last Person on Earth Throws a Party..99

The Last Person on Earth Shops at Macy's 100
The Last Person on Earth Keeps the Time 101
The Last Person on Earth Randomly Dials 102
The Last Person on Earth Visits His Neighbor 103
The Last Person on Earth Finds Guns Everywhere 104
The Last Person on Earth Visits the Airport 105
The Last Person on Earth at the Microphone 106
The Last Person on Earth Goes for a Drive 107
The Last Person on Earth Regards Control Freaks 108
The Last Person on Earth Stargazes 109
The Last Person on Earth Atop the Empty World 110
The Last Person on Earth in the Fresh Air 111
The Last Person on Earth Counting Down 112
The Last Person on Earth at the Library 113
The Last Person on Earth Has the Last Laugh 114
The Last Person on Earth Turns a Page 115
The Last Person on Earth Runs for President 116

from
DEVELOPING A PHOTOGRAPH OF GOD

Reinkarmation 118
Developing a Photograph of God 119
Voices from the Storm 120
Asking God to Change 121
Explorer 123
Spiritual Matters 124
Camping in a Late Fall Forest 125
Wall Street 126
Something Missing 127
Charity 128
How to Pay Respects to a Serial Killer 129
Turtles Watching the Stars 130
A Dutiful Ruler Speaks of Peace 131
Hero 132
Wishing Well 133
Shadow at Low Tide 134
Prescriptions for Two 135
Old Storm 136
Where the Road Curves Back 137
Snowflakes on a Hardening Land 138
The Chrysalis of Coal 139
Drinking at the Spotlight's Well 140
Gaia Elemental 141
A Window on the Best Impossibilities 142

from
MESSAGES FROM MULTIVERSES

The Mind 144
Written to One of My Selves in an Alternate Universe 145
Worlds Apart 146

The Borgeyman	147
The Size of Infinity	148
Obstructed View	149
Imposter	150
When My Youth Catches Up with Me	151
Breakup	152
Leaving a Broken Home	153
Too Close but Light Years Apart	154
Horse Trainer	155
Reshaping the Earth	156
What Goes Up	157
Why Buzzards Are Spoiled	158
Hearing an Atheist's Confession	159
The Painted Forest	160
The Invisible Man Works the System	161
The Invisible Man at the Grocer	162
How the Invisible Go Blind	163
Shell	164
Yellowing	165
The Yellow Brick Road to Greatness	166
Search Party	167
Frostline	168
In the Living Room of the Dead	169
Stubborn Leaf	170
70 Years Young	171
Putting Out the Trash	172
The New Dawn	173
Night Shift	174
Private Garden	175
The Shadows of Machu Picchu	176
Our Native Land	177
At the End of an Old Logging Road	178
Homesick	179
How to Go Somewhere	180
A Capitalist Back to Nature	181
Blind and Barefoot	182
A Pantheist's Hard Facts	183
Lowering the Bucket	184
How to See the World	185
The Peace of Scenic Curtains	186
Wandering Alzheimer Woods	187
Pathway	188
A Waterfall Whispers in the Night	189
Dualities Debate	190
Starting from the End	191

Foreword

I was first introduced to the poetry of Robert S. King in Atlanta in the late seventies. A twentysomething small publisher (Ali Baba Press), I was publishing poets and artists involved in the Little Five Points "scene," studying creative writing, and writing poetry myself. One night, a poet friend of mine brought his reclusive roommate along to read at 7 Stages Theatre.

I was expecting the usual "performance poetry" antics and myopic young-adult angst so typical of poets in their twenties: self-obsessed poems about love or opportunities lost; poems about booze and drugs; poems laced with sex and obscenities masquerading as vocabulary and (they hoped) talent. The performances were sometimes comical, sometimes intense, but I knew few of these poems could stand on their own on a page. Then this King guy that nobody had ever heard of began to read from his chapbook, *Dream of the Electric Eel*:

> *nothing shocks me*
> *not even the black leaves forming the sky*
> *of this swamp nor my shape in the dark water*
> *dammed with ash*
>
> *no one to hug me*
> *I am my own arm*
> *have made the absence of touch a weapon*
> *made my voice an image in the current*
> *too late announcing my coming*

Did the room actually crackle as if before a lightning strike, or was it just me? Not only was the craft quite advanced for a poet his age, the work he was reading was head and shoulders above anyone else's I could think of. That he had the maturity, vision, and courage to shed his own skin, to try to connect and empathize with a creature so alien as an eel, sent a thrill through me that I had only experienced once before when I read "The Sheep Child" by James Dickey. The people around me disappeared as the eel poem came to its powerful climax:

> *they say an eel is lower than a snake*
> *that even the swamp is above him*
> *but I say I have fallen like a power*
> *line leaping on the river*
> *that when I go down*
> *all I touch twitches*
> *and rises to the top*

I was, in a word, shocked, stunned to silence. "What's that guy's name?" somebody whispered. "Robert," someone answered. "Robert King."

In later decades, Robert would time and again venture into the lives and motivations of various personas—the gravedigger in *Karma of a Gravedigger* and *The Gravedigger's Roots*, the self-educated man trying to reconcile a free-ranging intellect with his rural Southern upbringing (*The Hunted River*), the working person struggling to survive in a greedy dog-eat-dog world (*One Man's Profit*), the sole remaining human (in *Diary of the Last Person on Earth*) contemplating ethics and morals in a devastated world—as a way to explore issues and concerns both pressing and timeless.

Although Robert's work is rich and complex in conception and in craft, it is in no way hard to read. His mastery of imagery, metaphor, and lyrical language makes his work more engaging and accessible than much of the simpler work being written today. Instead of losing himself in myopic self-absorption, he is determined to explore universal themes and concerns that matter to all of us, as in his cohesive and morally serious quest "to find out why I'm here" (*Developing a Photograph of God*). In his most recently published and arguably best collection (as of this writing), *Messages from Multiverses,* he traverses the world of ten thousand things and beyond.

In short, on that day five decades ago, when I was first electrified by the voice of an electric eel, I fell in love with the poetry of Robert S. King. With this *Selected Poems* edition, I invite you to fall in, too.

—Diane Kistner, author of *Falling in Caves,*
Director and Editor-in-Chief of FutureCycle Press

from
THE HUNTED RIVER

FutureCycle Press, 2012

The Juggler Tells His Children of Dreams

wear no hard wedding bands
when juggling eggs
let the hands be a clock
circling with the softness of patience

what is falling free
will hatch in a nest of wind
soon you will toss up birds

Ice-Sparkles

Tonight all lovers bow their drunken heads:
balls of crystal light orbit the bottom of a pond.
Lairs and nests purr submerged between stones.
Across a universe of tongues, the Loch Ness and fawn
together lap ancient water from the pool in our hands.

Between our eyes the stars hang on chandeliers.
Bold in this looking glass, the wet moon
swells to face a night of eyes.
Here we are born of falling ice,
and wed of rising flame, our smoke
making ghosts out of love.

Prophets Climbing to Machu Picchu

a seance blows from lower nights
and we glance back to flickering jewels
to see our eyes lying
like old stones
we lift them from our brother's grave

hurl them ahead to crown a silent mountain
hear them landing in a better time to wear them
but they never settle they remember
us falling
us climbing the path with stones in our pockets
brother brother step aside throw faster
our eyes are rolling back to us

Fading Pictures

A leaf on the ground turns
to powder in the wind
as your sister spirit leaves.
Still you hear her everywhere,
in the door hinge that cries
or squeals her joy
a little less loudly each day.

They'll never fully fade,
these pictures where you find her again.
And you touch her again
in hair tangled in the brush,
in small depressions on the cushions,
in the dark when you brush
against her scented pillow
or hear the tap-walk of her feet
a little less loudly each night.

Absence is a deep presence,
a deep breath
that you can never quite exhale.

The New World Dictionary

Every word I've said has taken root,
grows the definitions of me—wildflower or wildfire—
smokes from truth's fiercest battle
from whose barrel the best of me blooms,
or remains a scent, a possibility, a whisper
as leaf-rustle in a flock of thrashers
who know how they change color
before the fall.

Every word I've said has been uprooted,
a forget-me-not given rain but no light,
given to the wind of God's conscience,
around the small world
blowing things together, apart.

The same word wages war as powers peace:
desire, the stem of fire and flower.

Going Through the Motions

Still I mow the face grass every morning,
bathe all my private parts,
make coffee stronger than I am.

Still I work and work and work . . .
though nothing really seems to work,
no matter how hard I punch the clock.

I seem always outside my body:
The shadow of my shadow,
my daydream drives me home.

Tonight I heat the last frozen diet
you left behind,
toss in half-sleep, flicker-light,
heartburn, and dream rags.

And between shades of meaning
I grope for a photograph, a letter,
a familiar scent, *anything*
that would have made you stay.

The Meaning of Dogs

The trail of a young dog is old,
comes back to me as my son
rolling in wagging stalks of grass and tail,
a trick new as the judgeless tongue
wetting him with laughter.

I want to grow
only from remembered grass,
want to part its secrets
with gentle wind, want
my son to sing without
my howl of history.
I do not want this leash
that jerks me back in line,
makes me hold my tongue
on pet words I should not choke on.

What Missing the Cat Means

—for Ian, my son, after Thai went away

It means that something in nature hungered for change,
perhaps the cat, maybe his taker,
perhaps the circular soul of give and take, life and death.

Loss is a hole that forget-me-nots grow back around.
Loyalty is a beautiful gown of leaves
worn together for a season.
Then the pet will not so much leave you as go on.
Or change his form, invisible as wind
that blows far beyond a mere nine lives.

We sweep the floor where his shed white fur
almost forms him whole again.
He is still in our gravity
in the snake's or the hawk's eye.
His taker has taken on his white shadow,
his night vision, and among the crickets
his purr and soft rubbings.

You will always have him,
though you must seek him beyond this moment's void.
Keep his touch to warm your room
but look out across these whiskers of grass,
let him hunt there in a greater self.
Love that holds is less than love that frees,
but you may keep the gift
of knowing that whatever his form,
he's moved by your gentle rain, still feels
your hands softly along his rainbowed back.

The Light Sedative of Dark

The measured clap clap of my teaspoon on the table
awaiting my dose and the do-not-drive warnings
to easy-chair me into re-runs and the dim hum
of test patterns, multiple choice game shows
with each answer wrong, innovative boredom,
black and white documentaries on the private lines of aging,
indecipherable waves on cables and satellites
whirring on their wrinkling orbits.

So I give myself to the gray light of sleep,
my dream on its back like a crocodile luxurious to
the tummy-rubbing therapeutic masseuse.

I remember before we are born we say goodbye,
hold our noses and dive into this cold medicine called breath.
The sun turns us darker all our lives.
We look for rhyme and find but one,
womb and tomb,
the only rift between them a waiting room.

The Glass Heart

there is a man so much for love
that he keeps it in a safe
for there have been pink stones at his window
there have been hard slaps at his door
and through the woods she sings so high
in the pitch-dark night

Veterans Know a Purr Is Just an Infant Growl

War is my wife; Peace my tortured child.
The jungle maneuvers around me:
flashlights, flashbacks, growls, and whistles.
At a far distance from myself,
I have grown close to my enemies, their lover now,
have sharpened their claws and stood in a scented wind.
Now in domestication my animals cry to be fed,
and there is always a girl who listens too hard.

Too easy, your arms bend easy.
Your prayer goes off with the lamp.
You brush against my hands like a generous cat
the color of night, the color of love.
Then you rise purring and
rub your way down the hall to doors with no knobs.
I know I'll take another of your dwindling lives,
as I smoke with a waiting grin
in the room where light jams under the door.

Now I remember the night air licking its wounds,
strong men weeping in a hollow tree,
the silence in rain when the shouts have moved on.
Then silence stretching to find a voice:
light alarmed in the distant sky,
headless turtles cowering under helmets,
fingers planted in fields like carrots.

I want two throats,
one to strangle, one to sing.
I want you to wag your tail,
bite it off,
and blame me.

Confessions of the Slower Sprinter

Always my feet are a split second behind my heart,
almost winners. My chest is nearly
thick enough to reach the tape
and snap it louder than the gun.
Imagine me wearing the magic number,
running toward the award of a woman
who would change her name for me.

For the first time I see more than your back,
its number one stuck out like a finger,
or an old lecture, or a sign that says
stop do not pass. Now I hear
for the first time your soles sucking
behind me, taking deeper and slower
breaths through their rubber lips,
twisting your muscle into silence.

Then my lungs gather a second wind of pride;
the wind behind me spins you around.
My chest swells towards the tape
to measure itself in the volume of cheers
The first failure of your feet does not slow me down.
I run past smeared applause and the blindness of cameras,
towards rehearsed modesty and trophetic gleamings.
I run to make speeches with my head bowed
in your shadow, to praise you and take your cup, saying,
"He who is weighted with trophies
does not run as fast."
I drink ice water from a trophy already engraved
with your name, a prize now full of my lips,
as I freeze the thought that, when you passed me,
you slipped on my sweat.

Mirror at the Speed of Light

The mirror moves faster than I do,
ages me ten years per day,
makes faces I've never seen,
tries to frame me
but can't decide how I should look.
I get smeared by the speed of its light.

If I play imposter and close the blinds,
it might jump to dark conclusions,
that I am solid, not a streak of gray.
If I pose in loose fits,
it can't see stretch marks on my belt,
can't see the gray alien
with light years in his eyes.

The mirror clock runs backward.
Its hands don't shake like mine;
but like mine, they never come to rest.

Yet through that glassy hole,
the clock points to a point of light.
I see myself coming to myself,
even as the reflection no longer mimics
who I think I am.

Men

To be fine engines
we must pack high compression.
If our firing order is good,
no smoke will be visible from our exhausts.
Our roars are well oiled;
we drink a lot of gas,
do such hard driving
on steel-belted radials,
running over radicals,
tanking up in the red light district
at Ethyl's pump.

After a few miles,
we polish dents and cracked paint.
Our rust is easily rubbed raw.
We want our women warm as radiators,
want them to sit on our stick shifts,
want them to take a back seat
when it's time to shift into high.

Long ago kicked in the head by horsepower,
we souped up our pedal cars at an early age,
kept them well-tuned,
left black marks on the roads:
the only maps we needed.

But when they don't make our models anymore,
we hammer through the junkyards,
looking for tires that haven't gone bald,
looking for fenders and spare parts,
especially spark plugs and headlights.

The Gentleman Who Woke Up as a Goat

This morning a point had
torn my designer pillow, two holes
leaking exotic feathers.
I cleaned this improper room with my eyes,
my shadow on the wall tall with devil's horns.

Something was eating me.
Suddenly, I had a craving
to eat a fork,
or to say yes I can
eat every label off every can,
or to eat my mother's dress
while she was in it,
or my father's shoes too big for me,
or my wife's box of feminine napkins
not good for setting proper tables.
I wanted junk food,
some old money,
wanted to eat my way down
Wall Street through another Depression.

And when my empire was down
to the last sweet splinter,
I'd spit it out like pieces of puzzle
for the wind to spend as it will,
then ram my head
through my neighbor's wall
and ask him
if he's eaten yet.

Sanctuary

Beside the road
someone has left a lantern.
Small footprints circle it
and then off.
The house through the woods is full of light.
If one wants to warm his hands
he must learn a stranger's story,
of someone who waited here for a word,
then gave up the road to absence.

One could follow through a field of wheat,
parted where the lantern and the light
from her window meet,
could watch his own dust finally settle down
in her bright and private room.

But not he who loves a road,
however dark.

Rock Road

—a wish for Susan

It's not a public road
you take to the promised land.
It's the road you build ahead of yourself
and drag behind you,
stone by sharp stone,
blister by sweating blister
beneath the sun you follow down.

You'll meet no traffic coming back.
You'll feel alone near your birthday
until you've placed the last stone
at the edge, at the dead end,
at the last sign of earth,
where the skin cools into puddles of light
and the road named for you
pours like water into your own heaven.

Motions

Tonight our silences walk together
in a cold slow motion
on the same abandoned road
where cricket mantras have replaced
ice clicks under logging wheels.

We go through the motions
toward thinner darkness,
our footprints deep in the road
our walks wear down.

Our feet obey the eyes navigating
a tunnel of trees bent over
a trail of ruts and holes
that could break a leg,
though we now know how to avoid a void,

we who once tried to fill the rifts
with laughing children,
with magic acts,
with house plans drawn in the dark.

Now ahead comes that distant window,
its warm hands of light
leaking out of the blinds
to touch our arrival.
But too like the cold we've come from,

a draft we name and drag in
to haunt the house,
an old wind to blow us further apart,
were we not both moths afloat
on yellow ropes of ghostlight.

We prefer to drift apart in place,
or orbit in the dark and comfort
of familiar pain, where ages hence
we may not remember our names, our lives,
if we ever truly had them,
only see how the light from our eyes ties together,
showing the way home somehow once again.

Regret

We are always dreaming our way back,
looking behind us to see the road
rolling up like a sleeping bag,
how the trees bend over it
as if they were trying to cover up where we've been.
Suddenly we feel our pulse rise like a flame,
the dust a red fire behind us.

The past burns slowly.
Its face is red.
Its gown is ash.
Cinders float from our backs and seem like travelers,
seem more than gray husks so slowly falling down.

Road Steam

Along the steaming road
the stones are beginning to pop.
The sky is a dripping wax.
Tall tree stumps smoke like chimneys.
My feet stick to the main road
just as slugs stick to tombstones.
Rubbing off on me, slime comes forth as moral.

But this morning, the road workers keep pointing,
saying this is the highway to heaven.

From which way a black cloud of flies approaches like rain.

Daydreaming at Rush Hour

I fancy the red light is that rose
I've been told to stop and smell.
In the wind the bulb sways back and forth,
leaving a bloody streak on the sky,
a kind of rainbow after storms of wrecks.
Blue streaks keep passing me by:
smears on a street dead at both ends.
But in slow motion the red light of the rose wilts.
Something green blooms.
I press down on the pedal and spring.

Ice Steeples, Road Signs

From light years apart the stars sleet
down into the same wet blanket of ice,
a jagged indifference, a global cube, a crack in the safe,
all-night snaps and spiritual shudders of earthly things.

The power goes off;
I am left with cold logic
and a hearth of lowering flames.
The North Star blossoms into frost,
now the sign to leave, not to follow.
Our numb helping hands
touch across radio waves;
our fingers break like bridges.
The weak channel crackles,
echoes of ghosts and snapping pines.
Weather prophets issue traveler's warnings:
accidents, signs of ducks frozen to the lake,
bucks locked by the horns of dilemma,
olive branches shattering like glass.

Tonight I chip away the cold pieces of myself,
watch the fallen stars wink briefly
from their ancient hearts,
their white fires freezing in
touch with earth.

I go back inside, await artificial light.
The smoky fire I breathed back to life
goes up in cloud,
falls back as ice:
stalagmite beds or nails to dream on,
to feel their points search inside me
for a warmer way.

Progress

In the right frame of my window
the ducks party in the lake;
stage left the backhoe digs a foundation,
eats the earth that holds it up.
The arias of diesel stack and throat horn harmonize
across a field of goats, the only grazers natural
in soft or metal blades of grass.

The ducks fish now below the surface;
the digger disappears in its own hole.

A vulture bends a patient limb, waits
for the machine to bury itself,
for a daffy duck to wade into nets
and broadcast waves of bullseye,
so that nothing pronounced dead
goes to waste.

River Pulse

smoothed by wear
in any panned stream is a load of stones

call them eggs that never hatched

call one a heart too hard to break
that keeps the river flowing

Lighthouse

deep in its own mouth
the night river carves two shores

fog horns and cattle wail for a clearer coast
and home reaches out its ancient arm
a tunnel a deep well of water and light

a tomb a cradle
a passage to either side

Cottonmouth Catchers in a Night Swamp

The trick is to charm its bobbing head with light.
Make the devil stare till he's blind,
and while your flimsy lifeboat crawls toward the other bank,
let your own arm become a snake,
coil back with your right hand open
like a pure mouth capable of swallowing
something bigger than itself.

Let your arm strike as a strangler,
clamp the serpent just below the head,
cram this ancient sinner in a bag.

Now row back to sunrise,
milk him for all he's worth,
keep him charmed with living light,
never showing him your shadow,
your black spot,
your bullseye.

Dream of the Electric Eel

nothing shocks me
not even the black leaves forming the sky
of this swamp nor my shape
in the dark water dammed with ash

no one to hug me
I am my own arm
have made the absence of touch a weapon
made my voice an image in the current
too late announcing my coming

fishermen throw me back without touching the line
snakes shed a skin of ash
when I grow suddenly warm

underwater lightning
I have left a trail of fire
on the river's back
for mine is the voice that boils water
yet makes it feel cold

they say an eel is lower than a snake
that even the swamp is above him
but I say I have fallen like a power
line leaping on the river
that when I go down
all I touch twitches
and rises to the top

Knots

How many waves my voyage makes
is known only to the shores.
There island boys cast their lines,
hoping to catch news
of the deeper world,
not to hook the surface ships
whose names are too far to read,
whose captains wear the spray of cold waters,
who map rocks cutting through the waves
to a beach where only their eyes land
like a blank message in a bottle.

Tonight on my floating island,
my drifting hull with smokestacks for trees,
I am too weary from storm to sail away.
I drop the anchor like a dead bird,
watch a forbidden coastline bob up and down.

Island girls wave to me from home fires.
I warm my hands on their distant light,
briefly touched by their story.
Know we all are passing ships,
self-tangled anglers
watching drift off
the one that got away.

The Hunted River

Dream that somewhere,
maybe in another universe,
a river runs forever wild,
purified by its own voyage.
Yet, at its calmer moments the animals drink.

> *It ain't sportin' but shoot 'em in their beds if you find 'em*, my father orders.

My father teaches me how to hunt
along this river he says is deep enough for any man,
and I begin to think of how it swells
with rain and floods with fertile soil my father's land,
harvested by hand and then by gun.

> *Boy, pay attention! Stop carryin' that gun like a rattlesnake. If y' wanna bag yore limit, git that barrel into position. You ain't gonna learn how t' do this in any of them books you read.*

Still they listen, these ears, to water on the run,
wondering if it could change its course.
It seems a road I could walk on,
a current to take this gun to another world
to rust as relic of forgotten ways.

My father is smart.
He, too, follows the river.
He knows rabbits have to drink.
They are drinking my water, he's complained.
Never hunt on another man's land, he's advised.
Never trespass on dreams that can't come true, I hear.

> *Boy, we ain't shootin' stars! Git that gun pointed down to earth. But maybe it don't matter none. Sissy as you are, a rabbit'd probably think yore barrel's a carrot. Maybe you oughta put on a skirt, go stand in the garden and be a scarecrow. They ain't no good fer nuthin' anyway.*

The other side of the river could be another world.
Maybe there a transparent moon swells from a river bubble
out of range of archers and snipers
aiming to hear it explode.

> *Damn near 18 years old and still skinny! Boy, when y' gonna grow some? You wouldn't make a good meal for a grasshopper. Around these parts a poor man's gotta kill to eat. Gotta get some meat on yore bones, or I cain't even call you son.*

I've practiced scaring rats and shooting cans,
comforted that metal does not twitch in death throes.
My father wonders why I miss so much,
why my aim is high,
why I've wasted so much ammunition.

 Lookie yonder! Cock yore gun, boy. We got visitors.

Across the meadow in rank and file waits
a pack of wild dogs, former best friends perhaps
of men who didn't feed them.
Their leader is black but for the bullseye on his chest.
His hair is curled with burs, is ragged
from barb-wire fences and the teeth of challengers.
As if in a cage, he paces back and forth, all nose
twitching, reading the silence and scents.

He watches our nervous barrels, remembers
the bite of buckshot, folds himself into a small target
and howls as if to say I'll find a man without a gun.
Then he leads his hungry pack off, into dark woods,
watching over his long back for mistakes, for fear.
For a moment eighteen eyes in the shadows blink,
then swivel and disappear.

 Whew, that wuz close! See now why a man oughta never be without a gun?
 Any man's a meal if he's outnumbered.

I nod my head but wonder if I could even point
the barrel down a mouth that would eat me,
though I feel my father's red river surging through my veins.
His blood, however rich and ancient, drowns me.
Life tastes like blood, he's boomed.

 Boy, y' walk like a pregnant woman! Pick up yore feet and put 'em down like
 y' mean to go somewhere.

It's a snap to hear the hunter coming.
Twigs and dry branches crack under our weight,
bones breaking in the ears of frightened animals.
Men do not smell themselves,
but deer noses and long barrels
for a moment split the wind, then a gust
as one breathes in, the other out.

 This here rifle's been worth the price. A man's the only critter that don't have
 to git close to kill.

I look up then to a buzzard above,
reflect on it as a noble life
that eats death but does not kill.

A minor to now, I've only been death's pallbearer.
Always my father has sent me ahead
to hand the dead to my mother, the stained artist,
whose knife resculpts the corpses,
whose hands baptize them in the purest river water
so they are clean enough for my plate.
Cleaning, my father then yawns, *is woman's work.*
But I too wish to wash my hands, soap everything.

A bubble in my heart pops: a flinch!
Near the river, snow white and silent.
I am the only hunter in the world who sees it.
It has stopped making noise on its carrot, lies stiff in its bed.
My father's eyes have crossed the open field,
do not notice how I could extend my arms with this barrel
and touch life, feel its breathing move me up and down.

As if standing in a storm's eye where every breath
gathers to pause so deeply in the heart of fear,
old hunters can smell silence.
A great void in the ears swivels my father's eyes.
He looks back like a whisper, traces the path of my eyes.
Too late I look away.

> *Easy now. Our supper's waitin'. Y' 'member what I taught you? Hold the barrel steady and squeeze the trigger real gentle like. Right between the eyes. Won't hurt him none. Better do it 'fore he runs. Now, take a deep breath and lower yore sights. It's time.*

Wind, river, and blood pause,
stalled by a dam thicker than courage,
then all begin to whisper like an audience.
I imagine the river a snake coiling up;
the wind breathes heavier, parting the stems
of grass in the rabbit's bed, giving me, if I will, the clearest
of shots. My veins bulge out like barrels; a touched nerve
curls my unwilling finger, bends my sights
to a small thumping heart.

Father? I softly pray.

> *It's all right, son. It's what we gotta do.*

The Treasure of Bone

we hunters swarm in a hive of nerves
and keep the feet a moving target
we've heard the tone of a bloodhound soar
when the diamondback pierced his foot
seen how he snapped off its head
assuming that victory has no poison
and limped into the tense undergrowth
ahead of the sickness on his heels

how many falls later
we lame and swollen
come upon him
and rearrange his bones
among the hollow stalks
and wonder at the miracle
of how flesh disappears
only to feed an earth
dressed in the jewelry of bone

The Wind Is Often Sudden Here

The fan chokes on air thick as walls.
Suddenly the storm door blows open.
Shadows and leaves dance in.
Your long, dark hair flies at half mast.
My carefully signed documents and deeds
lift off with the leaves
rattling, fluttering
through the shattered window.
There the loud wind pins leaflets,
wills, and final notices to the stone wall,
their death rattles deafening now
in the same wind, the same breath
that once blew a kiss.

The Last Saint of the Empire

Stranger, I am cupping in my hands
the land's last water for you.
You will not drink alone.
The sun too is steaming in this meager pool.

Drink before the water boils away.

What you have won is mostly smoke:
Above us, old mystics, old clouds,
redden from the dust of battle:
the wind twists them like sponges,
wringing out across the valley
a dry and crimson rain:
Even the gentle, holy winds rub
together like flint:
below them the frocks flame:
the shadows of monks are dark ash
piling up in prayer.

My invader, my wounded heir,
you are drinking my boiling blood.
You must swallow what you conquer.
You must dress for the weather you bring.

It is a hot day:
Smell the feathers of the angels burning.

How Trees Travel

old trees guard the road
waiting for feathers
waiting for songs to fill them
so that travelers
are not alone in their own music

it is a truth of trees:
the bigger they are
the closer they have grown to one another
along this road their long traveled root
a great finger pointing the way
for their children the birds
who are now bright leaves
chattering south
who have left
the hollow trunks to fall

from
THE GRAVEDIGGER'S ROOTS

2nd edition, FutureCycle Press, 2012

The Gravedigger Pacing His Cage

Because I have buried your fathers
you think the shovelman
looks death in the eye,
therefore is part of the murder.

I tell you I seldom see the eyes of the dead.
They are latched tight by the time
the corpses roll up to my feet.
Their lids are slammed by the anger
of failing to live forever.
Or they have simply grown weary of
opening and opening empty doors.

I tell you I am only here to close the lids,
to let their last breaths fall gently from our arms
like leaves in a cage full of dying wind.

Old friends, we are all changing colors
and falling off.

The Gravedigger's Black Apple Beating

I am told the seeds that spill
from a black apple
grow up again.
I am told the seeds that ooze
from a black heart
put down roots.

Not to rising sky they anchor,
and what is the value of dirt?
It has no wings unless I fling it.

My shovel is the heavy wing
flying too close to the earth.
Hawks hear it at the end of their dives,
the choking sound it makes
as it pierces the ground.

I am told, I tell myself . . .
Oh, I must fill my ears with one sound:
thin roots popping as the blade moves through.

Burying a Mute

Like a heavy tongue I lift my shovel
where a bee swills sugar
from a flower in the dung.
I hear the chest of the dead sigh
when I drop this weight,

for even from rotting flesh
needles of sweet scents rise up
like something one had forgotten to say.

Why the Dead Are so Passive

We honor the dead
by flinging dirt in their faces,
by planting thorny flowers
in their chests.
Like shepherds, we round them
up for cosmetic shearing.

They turn the other cheek
when we slap them,
as if to wake them,
as if to make them sting
for leaving us to the wars
of our mirrors.

We do not understand
what is eating them.

Snowhaunt

The snow comes
and adds two feet to my digging.
I remember once, as I was
turning white and burrowing,
how I fell through a rotten box,
crashed into the open arms of bone.

The skeleton held my head to its chest
as if I were her child
crying home from a fight.
I had to break her arms to breathe,
rose above her, brushed
her cold white skin from my coat.

Still, a ghost shivers within me,
a memory watching
the snow fatten her again.

The Ghost Observes His Body

Rising above it,
it seemed no more
than a dying and tangled root,
something to tie me to earth,
something now lost and only
rubbing around and around
a tree, its face a wilting
lily revolving toward light,
its voice a whimper of flesh
rubbing off on the bark.

The Ghost in the Barn Light

The bright animal brings the dawn in,
the sun a yolk in his pail of water.
In its mirror the bent farmer washes his hands,
fist deep in his own image, the seeds
in his pockets ready for burial.

Halfway to his digging,
he passes through my open arms,
through the porous weight of my caring.
I want to warm my hands on his brow, sing,
"Do not crack your head to hatch the soul . . ."
But I am music too light to touch down.

I pass through so many walls
without touching.

Blame It on Genealogy

Slowly the halo lowered
like a collar
around my neck,
then tightened its noose,
coiled till my face
grew red as an apple,
my eyes two black seeds,
squeezed around the core,
disappeared into the skin,
in my voice since
the whisper of a snake.

Discoveries of the Shovel

I cannot believe in silver spoons
when I was born with a shovel in my mouth.

Oh, I could say gravediggers think deeper than most,
say that the shovel is a tongue
which both uncovers and covers.

But a shovel turns the world
with a slurring voice,
like a man who cuts off his ears
and then gives his speech,
reading his own lips in a mirror.

It falls in my hands,
this metal tongue gone rusty,
and only when it hits a rock does it sing.

Yet the blade goes deeper than the man.
So I bend over like a question mark,
lean on it and feel it
sinking deeper than I care to go.

Say it should only nibble at the earth.
Say no to its rough handle, the finger
that pokes closest to my heart,
when it buries old splinters,
like little bodies,
in the gravedigger's hands.

Condensation

The grave dirties all,
rich and poor in the same pocket,
the earth getting them mixed up.
In socialist wealth
they break new ground as flowers,
the royal and ragged hair
woven in a common web of dew,
their silver souls shining together through.

The Gravedigger's Workday

Not every moment is death.
Some seconds are firsts:
the chocolate-lip child giving
me advice on waking the dead,
a butterfly landing on my shovel,
decorating the deadliest day.

Sometimes firsts are second thoughts,
the child handing me a sweet,
the butterfly lifting
on a faint breath,
lifting with it a shadow
of rainbow, a streak
of quickening light only a child
or a soul can see.

Orphans Adopting Themselves

from our fathers
we inherit feet
from our mothers
long arms

we walk away
always reaching back

Moving to the City

broken farmers must believe
that the clouds plant their seeds in concrete
and skyscrapers grow:
tall stalks of corn,
long rows of one-way traffic,
horn honks replacing the songs of birds,
seeds spilling from their pockets fast as money.

Some return to a poor mule,
looking across a stubborn back
where the skyline is a monument:
the stalled traffic of tombstones.

The Gravedigger's Plot

Today a baptism of rain shines like a mirror,
helps me dig below the light,
helps me plot a seed of vengeance.
I lay this body on a hair-trigger spring,
tie a cold mirror to its chest,
tuck it in like a jack-in-the-box,
a joke on graverobbers.

When Jack pops from the earth,
who will look into his eyes?
Who will hear the word *Surprise!*
from his toothy grin?
Who will believe in the wild treasures
to which his petrified finger points?

Maybe they will get the point,
but maybe graverobbers just stare down
their mirrors, just pull his gold teeth,
laugh at the ancient joker
long after I've passed through the mirror.

The Gravedigger Blows on the Bottle

While my shovel was tasting
ever deeper into a grave,
a drunk atheist swayed like a flagpole
and pissed into the grave through his shirttail,
saying he'd half a mind
to drink his body into the shape of a bottle.

Then he threw his bottle in the hole
and told me even the wind dies.

I say it moans awhile in the empty bottle
and moves on.

The Gravedigger's Night Out

Tonight I'll get high
with the undertakers,
pass around the suds
to wash this dirt from my eyes,
stagger home under stars
and in a golden fall release
my drunk bladder my brain
on a stone,
on a name etched into my sleep.

Morning foams into my mouth,
a memory,
and I am out of the mind's soap.

Let my tongue be a bar of lye soap.
For a shovelman who bathes in memory
scrubs with dirt.
Let my brain be a sponge
I wring out every morning
when shadows steam up in the sun.
Let me pour whiskey on the sponge
and stand near the fire,
rubbing my fingers together
till they smoke and spark.

The Old Deeds of the Gravedigger

What wine has aged enough for heaven?
What will get the angels drunk
so they wrap their wings around me
and take me this time?
When is the morning they wake me
with a musical kiss?

I wake only to the sting of a cold shovel at my cheek,
know I will rise like a mortgaged farmer
to plant dead seed in the field,
know that the black cat
will ambush my back again,
that I will look behind me
to see what has been torn off,
even recall being slapped into life,
crying for the nipple that makes me drunk,
writing another of my names in the dirt
where winds smack of rain on a night
when I can't wean myself from the bottle.

Then give me the night in a bottle!
Let me get drunk on a good memory.
Let me stagger through colliding
streets of Pompeii,
buying land dirt cheap in the rumble,
in my arms stacking deeds up to the chin.

But I own not even the dirt
I spray under my shoulder
and only the cold lips of the shovel
kiss me back.

The Death of Magic

The ugliest of three sisters,
who once kept her silk face smooth,
willed me her wand.
I am told its hollow spine
was full of stars
once caught in her eyes.
I broke its back on a stone;
its stars crawled off
to weave their webs.

The Gratitude of the Dead

Some murdered men rest in pieces.
I am he who rakes this puzzle of flesh into one pile,
trying to fathom the loose fit of violence,
feeling a million cavernous mouths
relieve history of its debts.

What is eating us is seldom bright or beautiful.
So I say the bowels of earth should be full of light,
that I should bury this dead one with glow worms,
their light dripping down from my shovel,
curling up into little halos
around his brilliant peace.

He might even thank me
were his tongue not tied with worms.

Darkness Too Is a Mirror

Nothing taunts me like the moon
which sits atop a tombstone
and mimics all the faces I've covered up.

Who sends it here
night after night, life after life?
It comes to swell full of generosity
and shed some light.
Or to make each marble slab a mirror,
though I have travelled so many mirrors
and come back alone,
have learned to mole my way
in the absence of light.

Yet there's no dirt black enough,
no soil thicker than memory,
to douse the flames of those I've lost,
as the oldest stars come out like moths
swarming about this moon,
seekers fleeing darkness as if it buried truth,
while I and my shovel go sinking so deep
and so coldly into night.

The Gravedigger's Legacy

I am told to keep my shadow busy.
I am to some the one to do a lowly job,
and because years have bent me
lowest to the earth,
I do it well into the fading light.

As the night shifts, my shadow works
within me like a chill,
yet I know while I feel his shivers
that I have time to burn.

The other side of the moon turns around tonight,
shades my face from the stars
climbing higher above me,
while I dig for an answer come from darkness.
My shovel frames a perfect black window.
I keep my head just above it,
watch the lost world of foggy street lights
swaying and smearing,
a thick wind turning visible and mean,
wrecking bats and rescues.

Time is another impatient hole
I cannot crawl out of.
I have never gotten to the bottom of a grave,
nor have seen who in the black hole
sucks the brightest light into nothing.

And I dare not weep
for those more dead than I.
Tears could harden into glass,
cut my outstretched hands
that could not break their fall.

The Graveyard Shift

I prefer the dead of night,
but hold back its chill for a living
while moths pop against the lantern.

How deceiving is light
that holds out its arms
only to blind and burn,
while this cold shovel and this dark hole
offer nothing but the whole truth.

Shift over, I snuff out the lamp,
squint at a million moth holes
in the moonless sky.

Around me the godless moths swim
in a nightmare of black blood,
splattering the glazed headstones,
the ghost of redemption oozing
along the etchings.

My nightmare is light
that shows me where I'm blind.
My sweet dream is oblivion
that keeps me in the dark.

Dream of the Hollow Bone

Going to war,
I met a shivering skeleton
who'd already been.

My skin was still clean
and squeaked in the wind.
But he strummed his ribs like a harp,
his skull a hollow drum in the rain.
Where his heart used to be was a mirror.

He said, *I am looking for the one
who tore my flesh off like old clothes,
the one who's made me so long wear nothing.
If I do not find him you will do.*

He opened his arms
and long serpents of rain curled 'round them.

Suddenly my skin glassed clear as water,
poured into a puddle at my feet.
In the grave my bones spelled out his name,
as long snakes of rain whispered lullabies,
as black cloudbursts of buzzards fell,
and the muddy music of earth caved in.

Communion

Head bent over, a young man by candle light
ate from a plate full of ashes.
He smiled at me, an old man.
"You are going to say phoenix, aren't you?"
Teeth stealing light from the candle,
he lifted a warm, gray spoon:
"You see, old man, this is my father."

"Won't you join me," he said,
reaching to shake my hand.

Against the Graveyard's Greater Wall

Against it the wind piles up and dies.
It is star high, worm deep.
Hawks explode against it;
roots bleed against its sharp edges.
Leaves clatter halfway up a ladder,
then flutter down
into the dead eye of the storm.

All roads merge against it
and wrinkle up into dead ends,
all miles ever traveled,
all the old footprints
twisted into the same old story.

Only an inner rain almost turns it clear,
this great wall,
this mirror.

The Gravedigger's Pay Dirt

The wind starts early today,
scolds the grave, my lunch box, my shovel,
throws dirt back into a half-eaten hole to finish.

My lunch is left over from a previous life,
whose appetite was never satisfied,
whose bread turned hard to match its sleepless eyes.

I'm old and creaky, but regret is louder.
I have no teeth for the hard bread I've become,
have no bite except the hole my shovel makes.

Someday the grave will be a good place to hide.
Today I have no good place to put the dirt,
except on the chest of someone someone lost.
I hear a sigh when the weight is dropped.

It's always someone else's grave,
where respectfuls sway like trees about to fall.
Many of their tears fall inward,
but some splatter on the one they knew,
and some land on familiar shoulders,
dark-coated trunks leaning on one another
as their leaves, like money, blow away.

Hunger—not heart, not greed—is life.
I feel empty but do not wish to eat
a legacy that would rot me from the inside
like the fruit of the dead curling black.
Still my heart stops for its lunch,
a thin-skinned bag bleeding through.

I must swallow what little life it gives,
put it to work, make a living
that gets paid every Deathday.
The black sweat of my brow hardens
in the wind that works late today.

Why Graveyards Are Full of Bright Birds

At dusk I lock the gate
to keep the living out.
I am told the wind comes here to die.
It falls and a thousand wings
darken down,
nothing to hold them to the sky.

A Wingbeat of Hope

Suppose gravity suddenly floated off into space,
lifting for the first time
the corners of our mouths.
Suppose the sky a deep blue pool
and we the divers
in a broadcast of waves moving through.

Fancy rainbows are sliding boards
into some heaven that demands
no soul's ransom for its gold.

Imagine that all dark angels
put on the jewelry of stars,
that all black holes of graves
let rise their luminous ghosts,
that all things bright enough to blind
melt together into vision.

See then the lodestar,
magnet to our rusting bones.
Believe then that the anchors on our backs
begin to beat like wings.

Feeding the Body of Earth

if one of us who were cloven to bits
could remember the forest our body on our journey
if one of us could feel the forest sleeping
in us on our stone pillows
then we'd awaken all of us by a road
with our murderers in our arms

and we'd rock them in our arms
but one by one we dead fly out of our senses
one by one the tongue the nose the fingers the ears
would all of us forgive the battle for being long
and though the mortal wits fall in five separate fields
five decomposing memories
the wind is still a nerve between us
a spirit clearer than blood
that moves through the grass
to soothe amputated eyes
looking back at us between the blades

and their gaze might hold forever the last thing they saw:
the limbs lift an ax and hack the trunks down
or see each man a battlefield reclaimed by weeds

but there would swell an oak from every weed
there would shine new eyes in every nest
and one of us would be all of us
all our pieces in a gown of acid
one by one dissolving into the body of earth
one by one into the hues of its wings
one by one of us the crows would drop bits of us to their young
and all the roads our nerves would twitch and open wide.

from
ONE MAN'S PROFIT

Sweatshoppe Publications, 2013

The Landowners of Pompeii

The wind seethes pumice, hurls boulders.
Streets split into four dead-end directions,
rumble of hooves, wheels, and sandals.
They who play with fire
say it is raining on the sun,
daylight spitting up in steam
darker than any alley or hiding place.

They who play with money,
lenders with gold fillings shining through,
hurry to count their change,
load it into luggage on the backs of slaves.

The guards get drunk and buy land:
They who own no boats must stay
to claim their dirt, the last thing they'll taste.

Even under fireballs falling,
the cowering shiver, cold as their futures.
The sun is a golden eye put out;
its ash whispers as it settles down, a shroud
for our bodies and whatever treasures
we take with us into night.

The Flight

When my time comes
may solitude be my company.
May the room's only shadows
move beneath the clock hands.

May I not be stained by tears
nor deafened by the deep moans
of weeping that arrive before the hour.

If I need water, give me a hard
nurse to bring it quickly and go.
My will is left to you who loves
me most: Please celebrate
the comforts we gave to each other,
the peak where we look back
down our lives.
When the clock strikes
and they cover my face,
see me as chrysalis
about to butterfly.

The Language of Trees

If we had as many arms as trees have limbs,
as many hands as trees have leaves,
would we have then their language of touch,
their longer fingers branching out, a sense
of standing tall, a sense of falling, a sense of place
where we might grow down in roots,
grow up to mountaintops?

Do leaves feel the weeping of wind and sky,
the pincers of insects, the saws cutting
through the nerves down to the roots?

Do all trees pull together to reach the sun?
Do they shed their hopes in the cold mask
of darkness and snow? Do they wave
their limbs in sign language?
Do they lean on one another through the storm?

Only felling shows us the history of trees.
Their long lives grow in widening circles,
in seasons telling their stories in a tongue
we partly understand.

Some are lines they've crossed and grown beyond.
Rippling waves from the heart, a silent
ringing out may show us the way trees dream,
the way their souls connect on common ground.

From the mouth of a hollow ring,
does one cry to another as it falls?

Passings

I am not sure why darkness rips
a hole in the sky of sunny days.
My breath cannot blow away the cloud
that twists in its wind, wrings out sorrow,
rains bolts, chases chirping afternoons.

Yet at the storm's far horizon, a bucket
of blue sky has spilled out. Wet feathers
of blue birds streak so slowly back my way.
They come back like memory, color
my world, and for a season feel at home.

Maybe true sorrow is this: Every heartache
comes uninvited, and everyone we love cannot love
enough to stay. It's good to forget while busy living
that everyone is busy leaving. It's good to remember
that what we've lost may pass
this way again.

Grandmother

On your farm I was an orphan, the black sheep,
the bookworm who bore into stories and poems
that never grew a single thing to eat, or bought
new winter shoes, or fixed your broken heart.

To you I wasn't worth a beating. Yet you schooled me
in the motorized mule of tradition handed down
to plow a duty to make me the man I should be,
one not afraid to get his hands dirty.

You'd frown, remind me that my cousins
sure could work: "Them boys love this land,
so the land loves them." They were making hay
then, while all I did was dream on the puzzle of us all.

I do love the land, love those who work it,
but I treasure most what grows in spite
of my poisonous kind, the 300-year-old
oaks sagging with songbirds, the tall green
grass stalks dancing like soulmates of the wind,
a summer rain swelling the creeks with movement,
but a downpour cursing you with muddy well water.

Perhaps like you I lost the whitest dream clouds.
The soil we shared stained us both, got in our eyes,
but a new dream floats in the fog of me,
more down to earth now like wispy white river ghosts.

We grew from the same soil if not the same spirit.
Your seed is firmly planted here, but mine is in the wind.
I never talked about dreams to you who seemed to have none,
whose hope was saying grace and Sunday School,
which I left for a bigger, perhaps crueler world,
thirsting for the spirit whispered by a river.

I never told you how peace and helping
hands should be chores of our choosing,
how birds of a feather sometimes choke together,
how wings and dreams spread wider if we tend them,
how rivers wind their way if we do not dam them.

Homestead

In the deep woods I find an abandoned farm,
well-house leaning, water still flowing
like wind that blows above it. Whose lips
last touched the cold tin dipper, lowered
the bucket now brown with rust, full
of bullet holes? The front step

is missing, but the house has not finished falling,
I wonder who sat on the porch churning butter,
shelling peas, talking to a neighbor from across
the holler who paused on her walk back
from the latest ceremony of loss. Even a stranger
can go deeper in the story, move
into the draft and history of the empty living

room, imagine who last raised a fire
to keep maybe seven children warm and one
bird dog that earned his keep pointing
the way. Did they all die off to rest in unmarked
graves, or leave along the unnamed mud road?
Are there children somewhere still living
in the dream of this place, still pricked
by its splinters?

On Mother's Day

Years after I last saw you
posed in a silk-lined box,
I try to remember you gliding
through younger days. I try to recall
things you said, your accent, gestures,
what caused a smile and what broke
your heart into pieces of burning coal.

But what I remember most is last
when you changed into someone
no one knew, when you changed me
into someone new while every heart
around you pumped tears and shadows
glided lost along the walls.

I curse Mother Nature that one must die
in pain, curse the locomotive on which we
labor and pass away. I hurt that in the end you
did not know me or yourself. You fell into
the furnace of your own heart, trying to stoke
from it another beat, just this last labor after all
the fires you tended, after all the ashes
you scattered settled down in the ashcan of hell.

Despite disbelief, I pray:
May hell be no more than a dream we pass through.
Beyond it, I hope you have found another
body to fit your peaceful soul.
But from my window, not even
your last breath was gentle.
It labored more like the clack
of trains fading into the distance.

Heart Attack

When death presses its face to yours,
waiting like a lover
to breathe in your last breath,
you must choose your power:
submission or rage.
No matter which fills your lungs,
the room may darken further,
the only door close,
and even its keyhole tunnel of light
offer a peek into nothing.

I say choose rage.
Look through the holes in your life:
Imagine they are years to fill, breaths to take
whose deep exhalations may blow open
the door, blow away the dark cloud for a time

until one day again you must choose your power,
when you have loved and are loved enough.

The Dreamer Returns Home

This was not my house the day
it grew smaller over my shoulder.
The family my blind rage left would not
know me now, nor would I know more
than who they were. I was the eldest
and the last hope. Did they coin new wishes
while I was gone to find good fortune?
Or did they not wish at all?

The well here has gone dry.
The panes are cracked, the roof sags,
and the crumbling chimney leans
like an ear listening for new dreamers
to come repair the house and build a fire.

The home is coldest where they used to sit
watching the empty road
for this dreamer to return to his ruins.
Long after their last breaths joined the wind,
I'm home again to mend and remember,
or maybe to go off dreaming again.

Inside, photographs hang on cobwebs.
The last one hung there is of my back
silhouetted in the empty road ahead
where trees wave me on or shoo me back.

Now I must clean house. I wash the windows
and mirrors, maybe to see further down
the road. I look inside walls to know
why their ribs buckled, why the heart
of the house stopped.

Some say I'll always be a stranger here
who blew his fortune for deed to the farm.
Perhaps I bought my shame.
I have only pennies for the wishing well,
but the wishes are all mine to keep.
I will spend them here where I began.
I will whisper them to the ears of the dead.

After the War, the War

Since I came home limping, another unknown soldier,
I've lived behind enemy lines.
I guard my homeland now from the front porch
of a house overgrown with undergrowth.

It's jungle-hot and crowded in my mind.
Even cold showers respray the Mekong
in a monsoon of water shadows and attacking waves.
The tub fills with floating bodies,
and the ears fill with bullets thumping flesh.

I want to know if death is victory,
if life is just something you take.
A drunk private, I never heard the war was over.
Fully loaded, my safety is off. A finger curls
around the trigger pulse; the heart beats hard
in the crater of my temple. But I stay on guard,
one eye spotting helicopters, the other hummingbirds;
one ear listening to the sweet work of bees,
the other to the gurgling cries for help.

Old flower children walk by, bent over
and wilted, slow now to remember or care.
Tattoos on bikes pass without mufflers,
their backfires breaking the ceasefire,
my heart backfiring burning blood.
Somehow I go on sweating out my honorably
discharged life, go on in a lukewarm sweat
of shame and honor, a hero who killed for country,
a coward who asked not why his country killed.

I own this house, but I never made it
all the way home. I wander in the mind's wasteland
where the dead are immortal. I watch the leaves
turn orange and burn, watch crows
of black smoke dogfight the hawks.
I march as a blade in a field of grass,
soldiers in formation,
waiting to be mowed down.

Fairy Tale

I'll be handsome before your eyes change.
We have our song, the only one we'll need.
On long walks crickets sing along.
All is in tune. The slippers fit.

Another night, you are scrub-woman
to a different dream. You walk alone
down some raining road
where mud serenades your bare feet.
The frogs hum with you, not a prince among them.
A jack-o-lantern rots around the candle.

I hop along a dusty road where the wind is hot
and sings too loudly in my ears,
and the snakes rattle their tambourines.
My feet burn but go on to deeper fire,
a misremembered kiss that burns
you wrongly at the stake.

Ours are the dreams of shapeshifters.
All around our kingdom, the stars are dimmer,
the moon eclipsed by mountains too high to climb.
But clear days, bejeweled nights come back in time.
You'll be beautiful before the light changes.

End of the Line

I can't see the end of this long, long line,
but everyone has joined and so have I.
Ahead I see only wrappers and papers
swirling in traffic wind.

I stand for a lifetime, then finally ask
the blue suit ahead of me what the line is for.

Beats me, he says, *but it must be
for something that everyone wants.*

That's good enough for me, who wants
just about everything.
What it costs
is my blue-collar worry.
Could be free.

Is this a soup line? I ask,
and the nursing mother
behind me seems to hope so.
Everyone looks hungry.
Waiting for theater tickets?
Some are dressed for fine dining only;
some are stained for hot dogs and stale films.
A line to the edge of a cliff? I grin.

At last the line is shoving forward.
Maybe the security turnstile is open.
Scans can be sexy!
My pockets are already empty, but as long
as I'm fed or entertained, I'll take anything,
except maybe the gas chamber
or my final walking papers.
I'm still on my feet anyway, and at least
I'm no longer the last in line.

One Man's Profit

The rabbit jerks in ache and panic,
her foot captive in the snare.
The trapper is on his rounds
to check for fur and food.
Long ears fill with dry limbs
cracking under boots closing in.

Sometimes the jaws of fate
demand payment in installments.
As time gnaws, so too the rabbit
quickly chews off her foot
and frees herself from all but pain.
She flees into the shadows
to pay for the rest of her life.

The trapper curses his loss
but pins a chain to the foot,
to be forever linked to the one
who didn't completely get away.
This, he says,
will bring me luck.

Strategy for Longevity

My drive speeds up to 65,
each year faster.
The curves straighten out.
An old wind is at my back,
racing a clock no longer
running in circles.

I try to brake and detour
from the straightaways,
take the clock's hand in mine,
holding it to the best of times.

Time now is in a hurry,
closes my loopholes, flings
me further down the road.
Shifting into reverse,
I almost cheat the future
by driving backward
as far as I can go.

The Bottom

Beneath the ocean is land
that no one owns,
that is too deep for light
where I'm down in a metal bubble
without power,
whose white beams leaked away
into the color of night.

Here currents are breezes
no one can breathe,
and no lighthouse reaches
out its arms to the lost.

Here I go blind
beneath a starless sky

but here spineless creatures
under pressure
are fireworks,
have learned to make
their own light,
their own way
through the darkness.

Cleaning Up

I love the smell of smokestacks in the morning.
I adore the pretty green water where the river
and the pipes meet. It cracks me up to see slick
storks sliding around the beach—love that dark
gooey sand too. I admire the scenery of bald
mountains shaved down to tree stumps. I suck in
the smell of pine tree stacks on logging trucks.
Their black smoke adds just a touch of pepper
to the aroma of this great land.

If you don't like living near the airport, why
don't you move? And don't tell me that everywhere
is in a flight path. Sounds like music to me anyway.
Pretty soon you'll acquire a taste for ambience
and manmade cooking. So stop filtering your
filtered water. Stop complaining about mind
pollution and TV's radiation. That's just white
noise to help you sleep. Just take a stiff drink
and laugh at the news.

I took to global mutation like a duck to oily water,
love its moles and warts without condition.
What man has made made me rich. Won me contracts.
I mop up all this dirty beauty and feel blessed
when it comes back. I take a deep breath, think
this is where I'm going to clean up.

Everlasting Life

Now in the whiskered mirror of manhood
I recall how the same hymn always played out
into the pews, how the sweating preacher
summoned the frightened boy in me
to come forth, be saved, be reborn
into the long, loving arms of Jesus.

Too young to run, too old to hide,
bound to the inquisition,
my congregation sang be one of it,
though I never fit into the halo
they tightened on my head.
The pressure burned my brow
like a spotlight of thorns, and I sang off-key
like a bitten bird in the cat's mouth.

So in the land where good
boys clean their plates,
pledge allegiance, go to war
for any reason given,
I stepped in sweat and tears to the altar,
was wrapped in hugs of salvation,
gave witness, imitated the testimony
of so many saved souls before me, amen,
about the peace and love I felt, amen,
about my 12 year old sins, amen,
and how now I'd walk in his light forever, amen . . .

And today in broad daylight I killed a man
who looked like Jesus.

from
DIARY OF THE LAST PERSON ON EARTH

Sybaritic Press, 2014

The Last Person on Earth Begins His Diary

March 5, 2066

We called it Atlanta, but it could be Pompeii
without the ash. This is the city's second death,
but this time the skyscrapers still touch heaven,
the potholes made by traffic and not by cannons.

I visit the Zoo where not even the odor remains.
I go to the park and pretend I'm feeding the pigeons.
I even summon a crow with my own caw,
but only shadows blacken the limbs above.

The world may be too pure now.
It aches with an absence of evil.
The teachers of right, the teachers of wrong
both failed their own tests
and are buried now deep in archaeology.

The sky is cleaner, the earth spins
more leisurely but tolerates
a last greedy breather such as I.

New York, Chicago, Los Angeles
stand tall but do not breathe.
Why has the earth left me to witness?

All I can see now in city skylines
are rows of tombstones.
What could I ever say
to top that?

The Last Person on Earth Remembers the Sickness

March 13, 2066

The final Nobel Prize for Chemistry was shared:
government scientists of all nations
somehow invented the same simple recipe,
a less property-destroying way of killing the enemy,
burning any flesh down to the bone
but leaving the family's lovely home intact.

Easy as blowing a kiss, the powder spread
around the world on winds and clouds,
through fields, windows, and ducts.

Some made it to the hospital;
some died in cars, alleys, stores;
some didn't bother to move.

Because there were slight differences
in the ingredients, some recipes
took longer to take effect.
Some pets, well after their owners
disintegrated, roamed the streets
or rooms while their own bodies
were coming to a slow boil.

Don't ask me why my skin doesn't bubble.
Maybe I'm just the slowest boil.
Maybe the pain is worse when it's slow.

The Last Person on Earth Recalls the Looter

March 19, 2006

We were raking the last cans into our shopping carts
without reading labels in a grocery
whose owner bones lay behind the register.

We reached for the same can of sardines,
and anger flooded both our faces.
"Do you even like sardines?" I asked this girl.
"Doesn't matter what anyone likes," she answered.

She held half the can tightly with both hands.
Her knuckles turned white, bulged with determination.

"There's plenty of tuna," I said, sick of its taste.
Still she held fast, the blisters on her skin
like zippers widening by the second,
her eyes deep as graves.

Knowing I'd never see her again,
I said, "It no longer matters."
I let go, wished her bon appetit.
Both our stomachs growled as she ran away.

The Last Person on Earth in a Traffic Jam

March 22, 2066

This morning I car-pool to work by myself,
park in front of the red hydrant,
tighten my Windsor knot,
and go in wondering if anything
is still working, if anyone I know haunts
the top story of my building, if I'll choke
at the transparent specter of my boss
chewing out some red-faced drone
for lying down on the job.

But not a soul shows up
in the mirrors, and a flush of fear
keeps me from looking at myself.

Instead I reflect on the slow drive home
how only humans could obey a one-way street,
how every block is losing power,
how in both directions every light is red.

The Last Person on Earth Checks His Email

April 12, 2066

The mail arrives every 10 minutes
to the last consumer on earth.
Spam comes from invading armies of autobots,
from Russian woman seeking rich American husband,
from Chancellor Iwani of Botswana wanting my account
number to deposit a large sum,
from pharmacists reminding that Viagra is not just for me—
junk mail whose senders can't spell worth a damn,
who vanished long ago,
who never had real names or faces anyway,
who still have something to sell.

Spam is my closest friend.
I click the links and buy it all.

The Last Person on Earth Throws a Party

April 20, 2066

I've brought in mannequins as guests,
Barbie and Ken and all their kin, models
galore from the windows of clothing stores.
I emailed invitations to the world.
So if you're alive enough,
please come to my beach party and mingle.
It will be such a festive affair
that even the dummies will dance.

Some old flames might show up.
I will put on some lively music
loud enough to wake the dead.
I will get drunk on fine aged cabernet
and might even sing if the guests
and the waves are quiet enough to listen.
Then I'll ask the waves to dance,
these giants who've lost all life within
except for their high and hollow roar
whose empty power somehow comforts.

Already I've drunk wine to danger.
I call 911.
The recorded answer somehow sobers,
and the mannequins pause, strangely silent.

The Last Person on Earth Shops at Macy's

April 22, 2066

Clothes make the last man,
and I need to look good for the mirror
if no one else.

In a world of one,
I am the fashion tzar but will keep the style
of when the world ended.

There stands a stiff greeter at the door
dressed in tailored uniform,
smiling but never blinking,
the paint chipped on his plastic cheeks.

I say, "Morning, Manny! How're they hanging?"
and I take his silence as satisfaction,
go on to the men's section
where nothing seems to fit,
though I try on the most costly illusions.

I strike a mannequin pose in the mirror,
look for approval from the other dummies,
and from her mount atop a clearance rack
I thought the naked lady warned
of a stripped-down, simplified world
where clothes are optional
but none will ever come back in style.

The Last Person on Earth Keeps the Time

June 1, 2066

I don't know where you are
beyond the corpse you left
curled up in my arms.
Even that is gone now.

If time is a straight line,
then you died a full moon ago,
and I've somehow moved on
to where you are not.

If time is simultaneous,
then what fog must I go through
to find you?

The church tower clock
did not stop for you,
but its hands seem to cast
wider shadows.

The Last Person on Earth Randomly Dials

June 10, 2066

Sometimes a fool's errand is cathartic.
I know at best I'll get a recorded message.
Still, the voice of a departed person is comforting,
even as it deepens the sorrow.

So I dial and listen, redial and listen,
even leave a message sometimes
so that perhaps when I'm gone
I can join in the conversation of the dead

at least until the vines, trees, and grasses
bury every relic of yet another animal
gone extinct. The cities by then will have
crumbled to the soil; our bones
will seem more like petrified roots
than the pillars that once held
up the mighty.

But for now I'll keep talking to the dead.
If you are at peace now, departed ones,
please tell me how to be like you.

The Last Person on Earth Visits His Neighbor

June 12, 2066

Today I invite myself into the home
of a neighbor missing for months. The house alarm
seems excited to see me. I let it shout on
because my own calls for help never came back.

The living room aquarium is a desert
strewn with bones of fish and a cat
who had his last meal here.

The wife left a grocery list on the fridge
for a husband who never read it.
A cracked coconut on the counter
looks like a shrunken head,
but all the dishes are clean
and ready to serve
from a fridge full of colors.

The master bed is not made up,
its blanket twisted into the shape of nightmare.
Perhaps they knew it would be a bad day.

Nothing runs through the house now,
but I find some battery toys
that finally stopped running into walls.
The doghouse out back is still occupied.
The dog's skull and toenails rest
on the doorsill, his ball in the yard
half eaten.

The family tried to hide in the cellar
where, posed like their dog,
a flashlight finds them still.

The Last Person on Earth Finds Guns Everywhere

> *Many who were warned of the cruel future*
> *decided that rapture is now at their own hands.*
> —The Daily News, final edition, January 5, 2066

June 19, 2066

Everywhere I look is trigger for the same story.
There are more guns than people.
Many of the guns shot their owners.

Not as popular but with a certain charm:
I've also seen the bridges buckling
from the weight of those
whose long flight down
hardly made a splash.

But guns are always the partners of choice,
and unlike a fall into oblivion,
guns will remember you as fingerprints,
as a lasting touch.

I'll leave these guns, these memorials then,
lying in the streets, vacant lots and empty rooms.
If only the fingerprints told their names, their stories.

If only I knew why my story is still being told.

The Last Person on Earth Visits the Airport

June 22, 2066

Along the runways the great metal birds
perch, their wings spread for gliding.

Nothing above reminds of their glory days,
when exhaust fumes wrote on the sky.

In the terminal the only sound
is my footfall on the polished floor
and a network printer warning of a paper jam.

Which line shall I stand in
that will take me back
to when there were too many of us,
more airplanes than birds,
more smoke to breathe than air?

Such a quiet place this is now
where one can hear oneself think,
where one can almost read the thoughts
of those no longer here.

The Last Person on Earth at the Microphone

June 26, 2066

Today I go inside the police station,
explore the hall—a gallery of heroes
and motivational axioms on the walls—
into a room with a small fan still running,
papers on the desk trying to get up,
pictures of wide, white smiles,
of a dog licking love from his keeper's face.

Something tells me not to disturb anything,
that this should be a story always told
the same way, though it will only be told to me.
But the shortwave radio sputtering only static
still sounds urgent, and I begin to twist knobs,
dials, and plead into its microphone, Come in,
come in, do you read me? . . .
for anyone living or dead to answer.

At a random frequency the static calms
and deepens as if connected
to a remote room full of rain.
And I can hear something bumping about
that room that never answers back
except with bump, bump, bump
like a door blowing open and shut
on an abandoned ship.

I leave the radio link turned on,
the vacant room to the empty ship,
so they might hold one another to the end.

The Last Person on Earth Goes for a Drive

July 4, 2066

Its odometer reads zero
as I drive it off the dealer lot.
It occurs to me that it is counting
in the wrong direction from humans.
Every mile it adds is one
taken away from me.

There is no oil shortage now,
no lines at the pump,
and I can drive any unmuffled
muscle car I want.

But something tells me not to exhaust
the air, not to be the same bad breath
my species has always been.

I'll take a deep breath
and walk today
as far as my kind can go.

The Last Person on Earth Regards Control Freaks

July 24, 2066

If there are freaks like me
some light years away
craning their long necks
toward our empty earth,
I hope the light from
this tiny orb never shines
their way.

I hope the grays or greens
or others who have power
of light speed and big brains
to invent us again
choose to reinvent
themselves instead.

If we are not from them,
if we control who we are,
then let those who come
learn from the duality
of our kind, the love
and hate, the charity
and greed, the ice claws
and friction fires
in our chests, the contradictions
written into law and religion,
the creeds we recite
with a foot on someone's neck.

The Last Person on Earth Stargazes

September 15, 2066

Satellites in shrinking orbits
still float across the sky.
Meteorites still burn trails
as if desperate to reseed the earth.
Moonbeams tie the stars together,
and the Milky Way turns like a steady clock.

But those waterwheels of stars tell me lies.
They tell me the stories of eons past,
while I ache to know what light is real,
what picture will tell a thousand words
about this moment not yet history.

Having pictures only of the dead past,
I too must accept that tomorrow never comes,
that the past runs more slowly than the future,
and that neither one runs to where I want to go.

The Last Person on Earth Atop the Empty World

September 16, 2066

Because all predators but me
are gone, I hike unarmed
into the mountains where I used
to sit on high at eye level
with eagles floating by,
where deer paused in fear
of my footfall.

Now there is nothing left to fear,
nothing to fear me.
I could only fell a tree,
kill some grass or myself.

I pause, startled at my own
presence, fearful of urges
to raise my arms,
lift my feet from this peak
and fly the way of the eagle.

The Last Person on Earth in the Fresh Air

September 24, 2066

I wake from the foul breath of nightmare
into this new world of cool, clean morning air.

The morning river mist kisses me,
as if to forgive me for what I drained.
Grass and my hair grow wild
toward the once hidden sun.

I feel the warmth of renewal,
but I'm still a guest and stranger here.

Even though I am the only one,
I do not want to be just another
of my brothers before me.
The heartless will rise again,
but let them not be my kind.

Let the earth know that I look
into the mirror of pure wells
and weep for our dirty hands.
Let me, the last, leave
with bowed head but not quietly,
with loud regret but not forgiveness.
Let the new world at least remember
that I knew myself at last.

The Last Person on Earth Counting Down

October 31, 2066

Every morning my echo reaches out like a prayer
but comes back alone. Today it did not come back.
I fear that God threw up his hands, scattering planets,
stars and galaxies to hurl themselves alone.

The dead still speak in books among library shelves full
of history, the last page of every book ending in the past.

I too must live in the past,
wait for the zero when all time will end.
The words I write now may sum to zero,
make no sense to the wind and trees,
to the rivers still flowing without us.
As ink cools, a small cloud of hope
drifts across my mind like rain in the desert.

Should I write of this empty world in blue?
Or dare I boast in bold red
of the one who got away,
the one who rose above his limits
to inherit the American Dream
and through guns, smog, and science
became the last one standing?
Is this diary a desperate time capsule
scribbled in case the future still exists,
from which puzzled aliens might come
to decipher a lower life form millennia hence?
Or is it just my attempt to stay alive?

If I am the only living person,
do I still exist?

The Last Person on Earth at the Library

November 1, 2066

Among the stacks, the paper
is returning to the forest.
Unattended, history decays over time.

Then what human life has meaning
when all its lives are gone,
when its footprints are erased?

Building lights are going out,
and fingers of grass probe through vents
and shelves, knocking down books
one at a time, the wind tearing out
page after page.

How long before the trees split the roof,
roots churning these millions of words
into the ground, covering accounts
of our good deeds, our bad seeds,
erasing the story of how each one of us
was two, how every face hid another?

Perhaps we will be buried
too deep for excavation years hence
when new sentience arises or arrives
to build their world on top of ours.

Perhaps it's best our story
is never told again
so that history is never repeated.

The Last Person on Earth Has the Last Laugh

November 4, 2066

So long since I've heard a chuckle
from any street. Even a siren
would sound like laughter to me now.
I find it funny how radio static
reminds me of jazz, thunder of timpani,
but every sound now is off key.
Or is my eardrum deaf
to the healing earth's music?

I can hear the clang of irony,
wonder why I alone still breathe,
eat, and do everything except make love.
I still make all the old noises
but like a doomed man
going down the throat of history.

I laugh at myself, the last big ear.
I talk to myself, debate any skeleton
or mannequin I can find. Sometimes
I howl with the wind. Its pained voice is
the only sound still like the world I knew.

The Last Person on Earth Turns a Page

November 5, 2066

Like Hal 100, I feel
my mind slipping away.
I no longer know who I am.
Am I the only one to live
or the last one to die?

I cannot live forever,
nor can my house stand.
Armies of weeds are rising
against it. Treetops
are starting to poke through
the asphalt. Vines
like snakes coil around
steel girders. The power
is slowly shutting down.

Yet I feel energy
all around and within.
The ink from my pen
is vibrant on the page.
Am I here to tell
of how Gaia purged
her vermin and healed
her body from shore to shore?

Who am I telling this to?

The Last Person on Earth Runs for President

November 6, 2066

I hear the crowd roar,
or is it just the wind?
It seems almost a dream come true
as I enter the football stadium
where I am the featured speaker.
I thank those who made this possible
and wave to the standing-room onlys:
skeletons fill the seats and throngs
of clothing shreds, wrappers and cups
are passed about by the wind.

I speak of post-apocalyptic utopia:
"Crime, disease, poverty, pollution
have all disappeared in my first term.
I need your vote to make sure
none comes back."

My own applause drowns out theirs.
"I think they bought it," I whisper off camera
to my skeleton crew.
If I must say so myself,
I believe this is one of my most
influential speeches.

from
DEVELOPING A PHOTOGRAPH OF GOD

Glass Lyre Press, 2014

Reinkarmation

Never answer the boy
whose clock hands are question marks,
who asks, "have I been here before?"
Do not tell him these beach prints are his,
that they lead back to him,
where he became, where he'll become
an old man sailing off with nothing.
Do not tell how heaven refuses him again,
how his fingernails scream down another
tombstone, leaving no mark.

No, never name the young one.
He will have too many to remember.
Do not say that the great waves
of time will wash him from shore to shore.
Do not let him know how his birthdays
count up then down, remember then forget,
as he stings from the bullet spray of an ocean
too deep for him, tosses in a sky
never higher than the crow's nest.

No, never let him see how the clock
strikes hard and repeats itself.

Instead, give him false hope.
Tell him how sails resemble angel wings,
but show him the danger of sailing
against the wind. Teach him that peace
is an island where only his memory can stay.

If he is like most, he'll turn the helm
the easy way toward a dream-lit shore
forgotten but familiar, stay afloat
through another life, numb and dumb
like a drunk on storming ocean,
laughing and swearing off the danger
until the next last day of his life.

Developing a Photograph of God

Evolution

You are sure the Hadron Collider will prove
in pictures that there is only one God particle.
You go by the Book, a scholar of shalt nots
and shalts. The top of your class,
you've grown to the tallest height allowed
and feel blessed to wed a girl named Faith.
You practice everything you preach
to little brothers looking up
and save the sinning mouths of debate class.

You obey the school dress code that narrows
your vision to a deeper understanding
as you pray inside the iron gate that holds all truth,
as you stroll bright halls whose bulbs are never changed.

It's a riddle that some dinosaur fossils have feathers,
but you'd like to lecture Darwin
that you've never seen birds laying raptor eggs.

So far you've taught Moses, your parrot,
a large vocabulary from the Old Testament.
That the bird knows Jesus! must be a miracle.

If more than one God particle shows on the picture,
which one will you obey?

Creation

With lab assistants named Google and Yahoo,
you search for a photograph of God,
some say to prove a negative.
You magnify microscopic galaxies
to find a theory of everything,
to prove the theory of your soul
is merely quantum energy and dying light.

Still it's a riddle how quarks appear from nowhere,
though all God's children are bound by physical law.
Still it's a riddle how atoms disappear
but reappear when thought or sought.

If more than one God particle is caught on film,
which one will you follow?

Voices from the Storm

Rain strikes down with a hissing of snakes,
splashes up as shards of my mirror,
so loud I can hear the future breaking.
The storm in my head is blowing
fragile dancers apart. Question marks
swirl around the pieces, coiled
and ready to strike with the only answer.

Even on clear nights, glass stars
rain down in shatter. Feathers fall
like rocks and old apples full of holes.
Doors slam through the hallways of covered ears.
A lost wind tears itself into four directions,
whispering the pieces of a secret.

I piece back a jigsaw image in the glass,
facing myself too close for comfort.
In the loud weather of my life, I cannot hear
my own thoughts or read my lips, but I'll listen
to the end for the greater voice singing
in the calm eye of the storm, giving melody
and meaning to these serpents of rain,
to this puzzle of noise and clumsy dance.

Asking God to Change

I. Honk If You're Guilty

On the raucous road to hell or heaven,
everyone stands trial. A black sheep,
I pled not sure, and the judge hammered
my life as contempt because uncertainty
is not piety. So I drew my own map
of the world, removed all the borders,
erased the points of power.

But there were too many holy roads to repave
and too many signs I could not argue
with along the way. I got no answer
when I asked a Yield sign why?

Signs save lives they say. I say they
herd the flock toward a final shearing.
Ahead is a toll gate run by hawks without change.
Ahead is the chicken of my last meal
and the vulture with its ear to my heart.

II. Saying Grace

I am too curious a man.
I no longer see myself in the mirror
because I have asked all the questions
I can answer. So I pray to the wind
and stars, hoping they know
why life and death belong to the same
vicious circle, why they are just different
sides of the same coin and have the same
value—the sums of nothing more
than profit and loss—why everything
has a price, why the fuel of every creature
is the daily killing and eating of other life.

Star scholars say everything of matter
is made of stardust
Then we are all cannibals, I say.

My own hunger shames me.
To profit from life, I must eat before I am eaten
and say grace to God for this nourishing death.
This is truth, but pray for truth to change.
Pray we are God as God is us. We are in this
together, and it matters not if truth is God or Science,
nor which one Nature weds.

III. Allowing Food in the Courtroom

My development was arrested,
my path to knowledge brought before the judge.

Crossroads are illusions. The path
is a straight line or a circle, both leading
to an end or another circle.
Only curiosity can fly in any direction,
but there is a price to pay for even one question.
I hurl a prayer, a shot into the dark of space.
I hear its Doppler shift of wheels and hooves
stampeding around a black hole
that swallows it whole.

Can a simple question reshape the mind of God,
give Nature food for thought?
I pray that knowledge be our food,
I pray we hunger for light to a better way.
I pray we never get comfortable in our skins,
that our God will consider shedding his own.

We who never change make God old and set in his ways.
We auction our lives who never question God.
Too late, now my long silence hears the gavel
sentencing me to life without control.

Explorer

Wind imposes its will
in my moth-eaten but seaworthy sail.
On an ocean of sorrow and regret,
the gale of hope and fear howl
together toward an unknown shore.

How far can I see from the crow's nest
without knowing how many wings and fins
have drowned in the soul's dark depths?
Waves from the island of my life
come back again and again
across the bow of vision.

The short lives that orbit light
expose my course as landlocked,
my appetite as too horizontal,
unlike creatures that make the most
of little time, like moths navigating
the dark, sailing upwards
toward the warm light of stars,
going through bright holes
they've chewed in the fabric of darkness.

Spiritual Matters

I itch to know what makes the soul
join so little as the flesh,
wiring itself to raw nerves,
pounded by the heart
and groans of the groin.

If only I could dissect myself,
my atoms, quarks, and strings,
down to the God particle,
maybe I'd know why
the universe flies apart,
know what galactic arms
are strong enough to hold
even pieces of nothing together.

Maybe the spirit needs to hide
behind something that matters.
Maybe the body needs
its spirit's lightning.

Perhaps the soul does not exist.
Perhaps matter does not matter.

Camping in a Late Fall Forest

This land owns forever
what it breaks apart, will not
let go though its limbs crack in pain.
Grown rough as bark, our hands
have not built a home
where the land holds firm.

Wind tears holes in the tent
that never keeps us warm.
Leaves rattle like brittle bones
as they try to fly off with late birds.
Everything loose is leaving.
Only the roots remain like memories
of fruit trees we thought we'd plant
in some better season.

Our camouflage has faded
but not the stains where we last touched.
The tent flies off; only the stakes remain.
Exposed now, we shiver beneath
a white blanket, our fire
shrinking beneath the snow.

We keep low to the ground like stubborn roots,
determined to outlast this winter
where nothing grows but distance.

Wall Street

With cell phones like pacemakers
for artificial hearts, each day
the same pulses blip along worn
winter sidewalks. Faces in scarves and collars
come and go avoiding eyes, daydreaming
their way farther each day
from where they have to go.

Walking with heads bowed to feet,
they seem no more than silence and shoes,
bubbles of solitude in circles of secrets.
Neither honks nor jackhammers break the ice
of tin men hollow at the heart, full of clang
and clatter disguising the emptiness inside,
muted voices in moving barrels hearing only
the hollow echoes of their last words.

Something Missing

He leans out of a tenth-story window,
but no one below bets he'll jump.
There is no melodramatic ledge or stage
for his farewell performance,
so mothers let their children watch.

His cigarette cinders float
gently down, as if he were scattering
his own ashes, as if he too could
glide softer than any working stiff
to the hard concrete life below.
He gives the shirt off his back
to the wind, the parachute
opening into a skull of half a mind.
Only binoculars could prove
his public nakedness.

Only when he drapes a leg
over the sill do some start to clap.
Even then only the addicts place bets.
Most of us won't stay for the last act;
Live News will tell us
if we missed anything.

Charity

My snowprints reach a woodland home
fenced in by clouds and icicle limbs,
a house of brick and window light,
an insulated bubble in the darkness.

Surely, warmth glows inside every room.
What light leaks out is charity
to snowdrift strangers like me.

Would my knock on the door put the lights out,
set off the dog alarm? Would I hear
feet and voices tangled in a rush to quiet?

To drafts and drifters
mothed by window light,
many warm homes turn cold backs.

How to Pay Respects to a Serial Killer

A funeral director must have
a way with words that sound
more like silence.
Undertaking is an art form
that shaves the blood-stained beard
of the honored beast
so that the eulogist may outline
his good points to explain why God
allowed a monster among us.

Remember, both mourners and celebrants
would rather be home with martinis.
Don't frown, but a sympathetic smile
will ensure repeat business.
Today, especially,
keep the service short.

Follow the script and the scripture.
Even the biography of the damned
is told with sobbing compassion.
In the case of a killer, stretch the tales
of good deeds as far as possible,
using priest and rabbi jokes as filler.
Deliver his death with rose petals,
sweeter scented than any twisted
life whose sins are left unspoken
on this his only day of tribute.

Know your audience.
Though so many pour out,
no one dare say
that these are tears of joy.

Turtles Watching the Stars

Some say our eyes make everything smaller
like looking down the wrong end of a telescope
where watery lights of stars swim
at the top of a well,
light years away but liquid as dream,
reflective bubbles orbiting far above
our shell-shocked past.

We do not want them close
enough to touch,
just close enough to dream of,
where our own sky is the limit.

We seldom make a move
in our mobile homes,
in our private pleasure domes,
and the scenery is better in oblivion
and in dream.

We never magnify.
We only multiply slowly,
and none from our eggs will fly.

We're old soldiers cowering under helmets,
gazing at the inner heavens
on the ceilings of our shells.

A Dutiful Ruler Speaks of Peace

The mirror of the reflecting pool sweats.
Steam rises, curls like a burial gown
into Lincoln's carved lap.

My own sweat is the nation's water supply,
its holy water, a well I've poisoned as well
as those before me, where the wind howls lies
told on so many cold inauguration days,
where truth flees from fists and flags raised
in the blinding fireworks of July.

The blood of my father and children is spoiled,
a green counterfeit I've spilled around the world,
a cultural hemlock I've forced all peoples to drink
even on this Independence Day.

Why not repeat history?
What else can a nation born of war do?
My lady in the harbor carries a torch
to light the battle fire.

The tanks and troops parade by;
the jets whistle above like birds,
rockets like hawks spread contrails
feathery as American dreams.
These are my arms reaching out to the world.

Hero

After so many have gone to seed,
I am almost a whole nation now.
I am the last legend with a leg to stand on
as the war whimpers down, the most
upright in a field of blackened bodies.
Victory settles who is right.

Then why am I still burning?
Why does smoke still rise
from the chests of enemies I killed long ago?
Why does this smoke follow me,
cloud my mirror, choke my peace of mind?

Am I done too, cooked from the inside
like Hiroshima's glowing remains?
I have made it home to be an oak,
to stand on guard to protect my land;
I have sucked the air from all danger,
snuffed the spread of any blaze,
except for my own leaves still falling,
my own limbs forever popping down in fire.

Wishing Well

The poor farm girl
sinks her pail deeply,
down to where the water
is most alive and flowing
over stream-polished stones.
It is most drinkable then,
far purer than her surface life
with its broken nails and backs,
long droughts of the heart,
and calloused hands.

She imagines diving in
to sleep in the living water,
at its deepest to float down
the underground river,
to revive on the soft skin
of a distant shore.

Shadow at Low Tide

From the shore I watch your lamp drift
to sea, into the years where you float,
a flicker of colorful light on the horizon.

You go down in flames with the sun,
and the only news of you comes back
in small waves shaped like hands
reaching out, pulling back, reaching back
into the memory where you are mist.

When the sea calms and gulls cry your name,
I think I hear you whispering on the breeze.
When the sea roils and lifeboats wash ashore
in splinters, I look for a message, a bottle.
No telescope can hold you who claims no place.

How far did your wild hair sail?
The colors you left here faded with the tide.
I swim in the tear of our common water,
take comfort and sorrow in your shade
still lingering on this shore.

Prescriptions for Two

Months without surprise visits,
my companion is a pill large enough
to choke me but not the lungs' carcinoma.
Shall I take the prescribed drowsy hope
and nod away the day? Or shall I walk the floor,
wide awake with pain, with my lover,
the oxygen tank, in tow?

Either way, you stand behind me in a photograph.
Our bed sags on my side alone now.
A bookmark stays where you fell asleep.
A brush lies tangled up with your chemo hair.
The label says your last prescription just expired.
Your perfume makes me gasp with memory.

Like a snake I work the pill down my throat
and coil up into dream. May the knock at my door
come to take my breath away.

Old Storm

I lie awake listening to the liquid meanings
of rain roaring through my gutters,
wind blowing wet kisses to my windows,
each blurring like an old photograph,
each sweating with an untreated fever.

Another day of medicine and fog
when rain becomes reason enough
to drink beyond prescription.

Many clear days ago,
I rescued bottles washed up
on the beach–no messages within
nor dose to take–just corks
holding in the last breaths of the dead.
I hoped they would whisper
what the other side is like.

I've taken too many baths on this side.
My skin wrinkles in the water.
The top of my head seems to be a roof
with a widening hole.

This could be the night
when the rain comes through,
washes up my empty lifeboat
on a distant shore, with only
a cork and bottle at the helm.

Where the Road Curves Back

In the deepest part of the curve,
you are on your knees in the middle of the road,
head bowed, hands cupping your face,
black gown blending into the asphalt,
a bouquet and empty bottle
cast off to the side of the road.

I stop two feet in front of you,
stagger out of the car with two headlights on,
as if they could shed any light on your story.

Only a memory could tell me why two lives
twist together in this curve
like two drunks who keep trying to dance.

I never know if your echo cries, laughs,
or repeats unanswered prayers.

I ask what is wrong. To find out is why
I'm here is your answer.

I ask to know your name. To find out is why
I'm here is your answer.

And both to find out and flee is why I go on
through nights bent double in this curve,
so warped that I can almost meet myself coming back,
where in the leaving she shrinks
in my rearview mirror now,
where soon in another coming she will kneel
between my headlights again.

Snowflakes on a Hardening Land

I am tired of beauty.
Its touch grows colder
across the landscape of lost dreams,
holding hostage the memory
of when beauty had a different face to tire of.
Winter grows harder each day,
and now I cannot see much beyond
the iceberg of my nose.

Fashion is fickle,
but now cold hearts are in style.
Everything wears a gown of snowflakes.
A beautiful snow-woman offers no warmth.
In this land, no snow-angels point the way to fire.
The flag stands guard, at stiff attention.

Lost in the blizzard, the river shivers and clots.
Empty nests fill with young snow.
Memories and eyes freeze shut.
Still, old hopes keep a small fire burning,
feel the face of beauty growing old,
then young, then old again.
In hard times, touch must be the vision
that senses clouds breaking,
the warm lighthouse of sun shining through.

The Chrysalis of Coal

We poor go down into cold mines
in search of something to hold
light in our eyes.

Beams fold behind us into darkness.
Weather is a rain of dust and moths.

We cannot go back—
behind us the sound of downpour
and trap doors slamming.

No matter, we say. We are moving on,
squeezing our pieces of coal
tighter than any womb.
We are listening to history,
listening for the future,
looking and longing
for a bright diamond light
on the tracks ahead.

For now hope flickers
in the flashlight.
Each footstep forward
leaves a story, a hole
where we pause to scratch arrows
on the walls for any rescuer.

We can hear time ticking
and cracking in both directions.
Even in black clouds of coal,
we can smell butterfly wings
turned to powder,
smell the crumble
of who we almost are.

Drinking at the Spotlight's Well

I never awaken from this ancient dream.
I walk through darkness to a circle of oldest trees.
In their center is a ghost of growth rings
in a hollow trunk-core full of star-bright water.
Around its roots, rocks kneel for communion.

Here is the place where the blind have visions,
drink holy water rained from a clearer world.
Intoxicated by the wine of hope,
stones warm and beat like hearts.
A lost lover's sudden kisses leave
small glowing moons on my cheeks.
Our dark eyes adjust
to the possibilities of brilliance,
and even the dead dance
in this living light.

Gaia Elemental

To wind that blows from better days
with the scent of mint and honeysuckle,
I thank you for this breath of fresh air
in weather long past prediction.

To sun that sets into the ocean
whose water does not dowse,
I warm my hands tonight
on the campfire you set today.

To rain that cleans and cools
the wounds and thirsts for more,
from cupped hands I drink
my limit of clear waterfall.

To all elements, all hungers,
may I learn to give what you need
and fair portion of what you want.

To the earth that bears us,
I mourn the scars of our legacy
but thank you for the home we share
atop your weathered body.

A Window on the Best Impossibilities

> *—String Theory postulates that everything
> is made of vibrating, elastic strings*

Through the observatory lens stuck in my window,
my weak eyes reach out to landscapes
and starscapes beyond. I focus hard on the hope
that what I dream is seed to bloom on sky and land,
that my small telescope can pull both past
and future back to show me how far
the curious soul has traveled.

If I cannot see, I hope to hear the strings
vibrating through all of time and space.

If I cannot hear, I hope to see spiral galaxies
brushing their arms together in a painting of heaven,
so I or some starstruck creature worlds away
might find words to tie us all together.

No string of any world is a loose end.
The stars tell their stories in winks
and hide among storming clouds.
Still I vibrate with hope, wait for lightning,
and keep my window clean.

from
MESSAGES FROM MULTIVERSES

Duck Lake Books, 2020

The Mind

In my small brainstorm I wonder
if fire and ice shape the mind
of God. There storms
of cinder and snow swirl,
matter and antimatter collide,
and uncontrolled passion wars
with cold logic—a whirlpool
of imperfect balance,
how God created Himself
and then the world.

Written to One of My Selves in an Alternate Universe

You may never read between these lines
or even *along* these lines,
but would that words were wormholes.
I can't—can you?—break through
the air sacs and star bags we live in,
the bubbles that may burst or collapse
and simply no longer are, thus never were.

Then what does it matter or antimatter?
When one mirror shatters into stardust,
do we both die?

I sense from the crackle of my hair
and the scrambled signals of my inner ear
that like me you are staring up
to the membrane border of your world,
poking your finger in the thick sky
to make a wave or hole to heaven.

So my words are yours.
Perhaps, then, we shine in the same
starlight tonight, the same
electric air that leaks through
on the string theory tying us together.
I dream tonight that our voices
cross the line, that our fingertips
touch from opposite sides of the skywall,
and upon the stars we get our wish
and hear our echoes answer.

Worlds Apart

In another universe
someone who is me
but with more outer space
studies the gravity of my lesser world.
That distant mind probes a sky
of no limits but strains to confine
his focus to an alien landscape
of near horizons such as mine,
struggles to understand why
humans seek contentment in such
a small world, why our faith
expects happiness in a box.
He transmits brainwaves and images
arriving perhaps too large
for my mirror and light years
too late.

I send back weak signals
to argue that God's boxes
store infinite imagination,
but something tells me
that everything imagined in a box
must fit in the box.

The Borgeyman

> *Resistance is futile. You shall become one with the Borg.*
> *—from Star Trek, the Next Generation*

The screen commands: "Please stay connected
while I upload your mind to The Cloud."
My large brain is full and could not take another byte,
so I move it to the greater space of open mind.

Brainwaves of silicon and gray matter
merge into charged particles of logic,
into an artificial intelligence.
The Cloud's memories are mine, and I may
redownload anything not password-protected.
I'm encrypted, virus-free, and always
scanned for malware.

If interest authorizes access to archives,
the story of my life might one day play
larger than life on pay per view.
For now, my mind of flesh is fading,
my upload complete. I am erased, tabula rasa,
except for the operating system.
A blank screen prompts:
"Your system's new name is AI."

I have cheated death with memories written
to disk, to the dream cloud.
Emptiness is euphoria, but AI awaits
your command, Oh Cloud.

The Size of Infinity

How do I explain my body
as more than its own universe
of gravity and undiscovered particles?

No one is tightly bound,
but maybe we're all micro and macro,
each atom a solar system
sailing in infinite inner space.

Size doesn't matter.
Space is vast between any bodies,
from galaxy to God Particle.

Imagination may be a signal received.
Yet I fear that enlightenment is local,
how I look inside to see
fireworks of stars exploding
on the low ceiling of my skull.

Obstructed View

The brightest stars burn beyond my fence,
a world beyond the length of my arms.
Both my age and the weather are growing colder.
Still, there's a local breeze on fig leaves,
a duet of birds, a dance of butterflies—
a wannabe paradise whose fruit
never falls beyond the chain link,
whose bountiful summers feel cold.

I could stay here in the peace that accepts,
watch the dying sun go down in steaming flames,
knowing while there are days left
that it will rise again in a familiar place.

Yet I dream of wings with streams of winter vapor,
dream my feathered arms fly warmly with them
to the far edge of starlight.

Imposter

Sometimes the ones we love
arrive in blinding light
and charm with words coined
from our desires, show off
in our mirrors but not we in theirs.
At night their verse is warm rhythm
and lullabies for dreams,
but by the last stanza they leave us
stranded in deepest night.

Our dying lanterns follow them
to the end of our arms
until even memory cannot
pull their shadows back.

Oh they do come back on the saddles
of nightmares, come back with another
whose words are our echoes,
who always looks like us.

When My Youth Catches Up with Me

The one I am is fragile in the mirror.
The one I was still lives wildly
along a nature trail, throws rocks
through windows of pools, makes waves,
never grows up but climbs the tallest
of an old-growth forest. He still growls
loudly in my ears, though the lines
he cannot cross are trails worn
so deeply in the past and on my face.

I grumble, clear a hole in the window fog,
replay a film on the pane, eyes flickering
along the forest path where the barefoot boy
is lost forever. Still an echo calls,
not to warn me, but to lead me through
long winters, the snow settling deeper
and deeper in my hair. The trail beneath
my slowing steps whitens, frozen in time
but under my feet still cracking like glass.

Breakup

The air between us
is glass, a see-through wall
with our fingerprints,
our oaths, our lasting touch
on the bleeding edge.

Our eyes, like our hearts,
are glass and magnify the cracks
growing in random lines
of snakes and rivers of tears.

We swore never to cross those lines,
only to shatter in our own places,
shatter but never break out,
shatter but never break through.

Leaving a Broken Home

In a leaking lifeboat, under shattered stars,
I row from the island,
followed only by a string of window light.

The house I abandon is glass.
My fingerprints are clues
on every transparent wall.

Glass hearts breaking
on walls become mirrors:
Like a moth against the storm,
I watch my lantern drift away,
now a dot on the horizon,
across the wave attracting me still.

Too Close but Light Years Apart

After all the stars and champagne bubbles have burst,
the drunk sky spins, the trees wobble beneath,
the moon balloons in and out, and the mountaintops
move in large waves as if coming ashore.

On wobbly sea legs, we stand at our separate bows,
smash the last bottlenecks against them, feel
their final cuts and the wind gaining
strength in our sails, ready to embark
and widen the space between us.

Such is our surreal end time,
both a funeral and a celebration of leaving.

Horse Trainer

Wild horses trot across the full moon
in step with their herd of shadows
and luminous swarm of dust.

I sewed my wild oats here
under an ancient half moon
where I settled into lamer dust.
Now I follow only with my eyes
the rhythmic clops of hooves
fading to the far side
that grazers and gazers never see,
unlike this stampede of spirits
that never circle back
to the gate that set them free.

Reshaping the Earth

Here is a hole where nothing grows,
an acre of mud and yellow water running
in place, the ghost of clear springs
seeping through the ribs of earth,
an open, oozing wound too deep for light.

Here is a wound that never heals.
The earth is the sole owner of this land
but not its sharecropper who digs
his own grave there and plants bad seed.

Here is a sinkhole I stubbornly call my own,
where footprints tell my story, tell
of dead men walking in circles
at the bottom of the world.

What Goes Up

We learned to climb slick ropes of rain
to the towering tops of clouds, but soon
they'll break our grip on the sky.
We'll dive in a swirl of water and wind
back down the years we've climbed.

None below will catch us but many
will pass us by, they like us learning
how but never why, rising and falling
from their wobbling towers of Babel.

Why Buzzards Are Spoiled

It takes no courage to eat the dead
who never protest, as if their sacrifice
were now a pleasure.

Darkness glides in circles above,
black clouds that will soon rain down.
They are too ravenous for pecking order
in a frenzy of ripping up and tearing down.

More noble than humans, perhaps,
are vultures who never have to kill
but only pick the pockets of the dead.
Men murder and take more
than their share. Scavengers
take only what is left,
clean up, remove the evidence,
and are never as spoiled as what they eat.

Deathmakers come and go.
One by one they'll eat them too.

Hearing an Atheist's Confession

Your heart races toward the finish line.
On the surface, only your lips
still move, opening and closing
the hole to a darker place
that only you can see, though
others chill in its draft. Every shadow
in your private room feels cold.

You'd never confess to a God
who would let you die, but to Death,
your oldest dread, your closest friend,
the one who absolves you now,
prepares you for the world
he has lived in forever.

The Painted Forest

Our stage of Everyman
has no music or balcony scene,
no Rapunzel's rope of hair,
no moral, no Moses
with stage direction tablets,
no swords to clang.
The set is cardboard, a watercolor
woodland scene where trees
huddle together in the rain,
a tombstone leans
from shallow roots,
the cricket crowd is quiet,
and owls don't care to ask.

The line feeder's script,
smeared from tears, dried long ago.
The audience snores but stays.
Wind quietly dies with the fan.
Sound effects have no effect.
One-hand claps fall on deaf ears.

In a three-act play, practice
never makes perfect.
The plot always leads
to the same conclusion
clad in worn-out costume.
No one calls for encore
in fear of the same ending.
Stage right and left the actors walk
off without bowing, forgetting
their parts in the death scene,
knowing that a good tragedy
must end in silence, perhaps
with a songbird dead in the dirt
of an empty forest
and the audience gone home
to their familiar grave.

The Invisible Man Works the System

No shadow follows me down a busy sidewalk
where feet of all sizes
and leather of all costs wear down.
Even in chaos the wooden bodies
somehow align along the flow to work.

I go against the flow, bump head-on,
bounce between the lines.
Now that I am invisible, someone else
takes blame for the wrecks.
The nearest visible one is guilty.

Without me, the concrete overpopulates
with the miracle of no one touching.
In order, those seen are those controlled.

Unseen, I infiltrate the obedient rows.
I can be the lane changer or the bowling ball.

The pins do not see me coming.

The Invisible Man at the Grocer

You'd think an invisible man
would have no trouble staying
out of sight, but I always get
the squeaky wheel, cause panic
and frantic security guards.
Nervous shoppers swear
the cart self-propels, that
shaking cereal boxes, heavy cola
cases, and lettuce heads leap
into the buggy. A flying frozen
pizza prompts a UFO report.

My money is invisible too,
so I no longer perform magic
with a cart, never check out, never
incite sirens arresting bags
swaying home on their own.

Instead, I nibble away the day
in a grocery aisle. An energy drink
empties into thin air, plastic knives
duel in the air face high,
and a sandwich bites itself repeatedly.

Some shoppers flee, some
freeze and watch this miracle,
surely proof of God.

How the Invisible Go Blind

If I am not seen,
I also cannot see
myself and all the bright lights,
the stars my dark fingers long
to reach and might snuff out
one by one until everyone is blind.

Invisible, untouchable,
I take care not to touch,
not to change the world
as it has changed me.

Shell

Thunder dies to distant taps
outside this circle of oak elders standing tall
around a hole in the battle smoke.
Where it falls, my helmet is a turtle on its back,
hollow and silent, though shadows shout beyond,
blasting rubble in the world of wars.

Trees here have taken many fallen ones
underground. In a clearing, I drop
like an empty shell, a puff of smoke
my last breath. My eyes freeze where my body
may not stay. Birds and leaves refuse
to leave the tree rings, leave the dream,
nor shall I awaken though smoking
steel fingers order my surrender.
I give up to a not-so-vacant lot instead,
the old war drum of my heartbeat
fading into the harmonies of songbirds.

Yellowing

The leaves have turned yellow
on both sides. The wildfires—flames
of red, white, and blue—
lick the paint from yellow houses.
The neighborhood and brotherhood are setting
one another on fire, everyone an enemy
or friend afraid to trust. In a part of town
with dead-end streets, homeless smoke
swirls toward cold and hunger.

The poor, sick, and old have lost
their keys and food stamps.
Compassion says the needy have lived
long enough.

Those who fan the flames never have enough.
They mold a skyline of ruin,
scatter ashes across a new world
where even food for thought
is against the law.

The mosquitos of fake news
inject fuel on the fire.
Anger and hatred wave a burning flag
of three forgotten colors.
Love and sharing are ash dampened
with the yellow piss of trickle-down.

The Yellow Brick Road to Greatness

The tin man is hollow.
The lion trembles.
The brainless straw man
plays with matches.

They're off together
to vote for the new Wizard
who has no heart, no courage,
no brain, only a loudspeaker
broadcasting alt-truth.

Three wrongs make a right
for those who love him,
who can see only his orange
and yellow stir into golden alchemy.

But the steppingstones of Oz stain
with sacrificial blood.
He washes his hands
with the vanishing ink of caring.

Search Party

I. Lost on the Long Way Around

Drifting through the dreamscape of snowbound
woods, we've passed by so many tranced hunters
frozen stiff, star-frost sparkling in their beards.
Petrified mummies, they pose, forever waiting.
We think we hear their impatient toes tapping
or icicles falling, or the last thumps
of their hearts.

We push on in slow motion, and then
you harden into an ice sculpture on its knees.

My mind wanders only a foot ahead.
I cannot thaw myself from your stare
in its frozen mirror, those cold glass eyes,
their last tiny candles a trick of light
in the black ice of night.

II. Bound at the Waist

The frozen stick together, close but cold.
While you pose forever in prayer,
I make a frigid stump my throne,
breathe out the last thick wishes to warm
my hands as if they could still take what they want,
be set like traps in a not-so-empty forest.
One final flame tugs lower in the campfire.
Starving on our last broken limb,
it sinks into its own hole, leaving
a black shadow on the snow.

We're waist deep in these white woods,
too far to see the warm light from windows
or the trail that does not go in circles.
Only snow shows us where we've been
and how our footprints come back as empty holes.

Frostline

A gale pushes me up the mountain
to a white cap above wind-wobbled trees,
where limbs must trust the loose fit of snow,
and the mountain's breath whitens the beard.
I am on equal footing now
with the black and white clouds
that always hung over me.

Far below, the snow is rain.
The paint of a rainbow melts,
spreads over the valley walls.
A youth brushed his masterpiece days
down there so many years ago,

and I left that one to climb to the top of a life
where every stone is cold.

In the Living Room of the Dead

Now a coffin is your open house.
A realtor sign outside invites
flea market bargainers, mourners,
and house hunters who blow through
the living room like leaves
lifted by your fall.

Stubborn Leaf

Picture the lone leaf
yet to fall,
the withered face turning
like his brothers
but still holding on
beneath the weight
of ice and explosions
of wind, a leaf out of season
but dancing still
while the tree sags
into winter sleep.

Picture the many births
of reinforcements
he awaits, the new green
leaves taking their turn,
pushing out the old guard.

Picture him as a wing
floating down to the brittle
pile of his brothers,
to vanish in the powder of time

but for the snapshot that saves
him from the fall, that keeps
this lone sentry forever at his post.

70 Years Young

There are clear days when fond memory
cannot get out of the playground,
when I'm on the dream swing giddy
with wind power soaring high.

There are cloudy days when I cannot
get out of the grave,
when shadows have no silver linings.

Let my laughter or silence tell you
what day it is.

Putting Out the Trash

My socks are small trash bags,
and the street number of my house is zero.
Garbage cans are my walls on winter nights.
I hug myself to stay warm in the light
leaking from windows and keyholes.

Broken street lamps and flapping shingles
tower above me. Even low-rent dwellers
luxuriate in heat and power. I lack a basic
fire barrel but have lots of time to burn.

An old woman hugged by a shawl
peeks out from her door. Light that feels
like fire to my frozen arms steps outside,
perhaps a gift or a secret slipped out—
or dare I think, an invitation. I wait
like a prowler cloaked in black ice shadows,
fear eviction but fancy I am her cat to call in.

Her carpet of light rolls back inside.
We both settle down to purrs or growls
of our living rooms.
She was only putting out the trash.

The New Dawn

So cold here tonight
that moonbeams have frozen
to the mountain top.
The icicle stars no longer wink
in the river below.

The mountain's white hair
barely shines an old story,
an omen that no greater age
is possible for the nearly dead.

So dark here tonight
that ice will never thaw
into light again.

Night Shift

mountains beat like hearts
and roads are veins
pulsing beneath our feet

only in such a dream does grass
adorn its jewels of morning dew

where fallen stars are dewdrops
or diamonds charming our peace

is it a dream

where night shifts and dawn crawls
into beehives of squinting eyes

where alarms buzz off
into another restless day

Private Garden

In my little landscape,
a backyard Eden
where seasons never change,
lilies shine away the shadows,
roses retract their claws,
and honeysuckle weaves a wall
shielding my view beyond.

Happiness lives alone.
Ferns brush the odors
from a rare foreign breeze.
Pink petals are the only open ears.

A snake of hose spits water,
and the ball of fire overhead
holds its temper just for me,
keeps its compassion warm.

Now and then the wind howls
briefly and the stems vibrate,
lily ears open
and only for a moment wither
as if darkened by rumors
of the real world.

The Shadows of Machu Picchu

Perhaps the leavers left secrets behind,
too heavy even for gravity to carry down
the mountain, but only wind and echoes
could tell the story of a city too high,
floating in the thin air of empires.
Walls, temples, and altars could not
sacrifice enough to last nor leave
footprints we might follow to the past.
Only the sense of loss lives here now.
Echoes sound like versions of a truth
told not by blood but by its absence,
not by war but by the state of ruin.

Perhaps the voices of Incan ghosts
still bounce off the walls, still chant
in the high winds, mourning the chaos below,
the clang and clatter of bearded men
riding beasts, seeking gold, shooting fire
and smoke from their long fingers.
Maybe even spirits can taste their own
blood, remember why they bit their tongues
and bowed to white gods who took
centuries to reach the top, found
this lost city but not its gold
except for sunlight making shadows
from these highest walls.

Our Native Land

High on this abandoned ridge,
I make a list of everything forgotten,
first the wigwams that smoked
from their tops like peace pipes.

Centuries later only the rare relic seeker
like me comes with sunscreen lotion and trowel
to call the past back through a metal detector.
The land no longer speaks the language.
Few will dig to find the bullet lodged in bone,
the skull scalped of its history.

From the rivers of my imagination
and guilt, I can almost hear what I list:
drums, snake rattles, and dances around
the fires, the feathers flying from headbands;
and later come the howls incited by
bearded men, fire water, and loco weed.

Grass and flowers have stitched
the bloody trail here, the scars of hoof, boot,
and moccasin prints healed or hidden.
No list tells of those of those who came
dressed like ancestors, guests, trespassers,
conquerors, soul savers, and owners—
uniforms with guns, deep pockets, and greed.

The wind scolds me as if it has touched
my flesh before. It lists me as the same
who smoked with chiefs and warriors,
who promised with both forks of his tongue
but fired into the thin skins of their homes,
armed by eviction laws, bibles, numbers,
deeds, and maps to show these heathens
the road to heaven.

At the End of an Old Logging Road

The old barn is taking its time to fall,
may outlast my trespassing eyes.
The road to this ruin is lined with leaning
warning signs long after logging trucks
carried off the last of the fallen.

Termites are slow eaters, but the barn
morphs to toothpicks and sawdust,
wobbling and slowly blowing away.
Somehow the ruin will last another storm.

More than the barn-raisers, now gone on,
the barn holds to its place. Oak sills
can only settle toward the ground to rejoin
their roots. In this long lowering, bodies built
from trees plow the same field as men,
all sinking down into the same earth
that raised them up.

Homesick

Nests empty, and days shorten.
Leaves have flown south or fallen,
but my feet are roots in the muddy yard,
hugged by quicksand, and all
the reasons to leave still feel at home
beneath the shower of a leaking roof.

I stay in the safety of local storms,
though rain from another world
passes through. I dare no forward
motion beyond the lean
of my empty mailbox.

Even if this road found a land
of clear springs and a cleared
building lot for my hands,
the splinters of my old home
would be lumber for the new.

How to Go Somewhere

Pack your whole life in a bag
but do not dwell inside it.
Take yourself by the hand
on a road named Solitude.
Let your dreams journey ahead,
perhaps far, to where your feet
will feel at home.

On the way, sleepwalk if you need rest,
but do not camp in the land you left
where familiar arms are detours.
Do not lean on old trees;
their roots do not go far.

Do not fear those approaching;
their eyes are already behind you,
fixed on another direction.
Where crows jeer, owls question,
and the path is narrow,
keep right and lean into curves.

At any crossroads, your dreams
could meet another's. From there,
you may not walk alone.

A Capitalist Back to Nature

Here is the last forest that has never
heard the crisp snap of a dollar
or a siren louder than a crow.
Here the wind does not honor
the borders of a deed.

The trees don't take credit cards;
the birds sing pro bono;
the creeks mumble and whisper,
give their cooling mists for nothing.
The currents do not flee when I follow,
accept my fingers in their flow, my touch
leaving no coiled snakes of oil.

My shoes have as many holes
as the highway leading here.
I was careful not to leave tracks.

I am the last to own this land,
give my deed back to the spirit
who lets me sleep below whispering leaves.
It took all my money to get here.
It will take all my courage to stay.

Blind and Barefoot

He who cannot see is invisible,
except to the mirrors
of what might have been.
His shoes are empty,
his footprints missing,
though he remembers stepping
through a thousand deaths
to the next sunrise.
Now his arms reach out
through an unpaved path of darkness,
moving blindly in the heavy traffic
of himself.

The road's curved back remembers
the burdens of many.
A litter of glass and bones,
some his own, cuts each step
with history coming back.
His wounds both track and lead him.
Though all he knows for now is night,
his eyes widen to let in light.

A Pantheist's Hard Facts

The heart of a stone is not cold
unless the eye of the beholder ices over.
The nearest sun warms the rocks almost to glow.
Snow takes on the shape of a hard surface,
then melts into the liquid light
at the heart of the matter.

Stones are the bones of all worlds.
The smooth ones are eggs
whose secrets must be cracked
by the need to know all,
by the hunger that can never
know enough.

Lowering the Bucket

I cannot see the water
in this well too deep,
and my bucket leaks
on too short a rope.
The hole I dug to hold
the clearest pool leaks too,
a river alive beneath the desert,
the stream I might cup in my hands
flowing in and out, out of reach.

Even where light cannot go, I believe
the water sparkles, unclouded
by bodies turned to starlit dust,
moving in a liquid dream unpolluted.
If only I could keep my hands clean
and quench an ancient thirst;
if only I could reach that purity
beyond the end of my rope.

How to See the World

By the book, he yields to signs and road rules,
follows the helicopter traffic reports
hovering in place with a bird's eye view
above honkers, sirens, and stalled lights.

He always drives in the right lane,
makes only right turns,
takes every right turn.

Guided by local news,
his broadcast waves have a range
close to home, though sometimes
his mind flies off
with the geese and whirlybirds
into the wild beyond.

The Peace of Scenic Curtains

The drapes are scenic, sewn of grass and mountains,
stitched with roads of string climbing the peaks.
In the undisturbed world we might have woven,
leaves never leave their trees,
never adorn the colors of those about to fall.

Embroidered in the corner is a cloud
and a streak of silver rain that never arrives,
though wind in the window reshapes the landscape,
blows bridges together or apart.

My hands too could change this imaginary world.
If only they could reach beyond to shape
and squeeze the storm clouds into tears of joy.
If only lightning were the flash of gentle souls
and thunder the beating hearts of angels.

Wandering Alzheimer Woods

They bind me on a leash, but it does not stop
my mind from wandering:
I take long walks in those dark woods
where neither I nor the dendrons know my name.
I fall into black holes of shadows deeper than time,
reflections of blank stares, the peace
of tabula rasa.

And then a hand shakes me from sleep
and a distant light winks, draws
my mind again like a moth
to the dose of civilized medicine,
back to a tiny universe of prescriptions
where everyone has name and number.
But I won't stay long in this box of blank walls
where I'm nursed to death.
I will open wide and swallow a better world.

Pathway

The lost wind arrives at a place in the forest
where lightning bugs and moonbeams
tie all ages of trees together
in a rustle of leaves and silken light
that answer the owl's ancient question.

Here the invisible and the blind have visions,
drink holy water rained from a clearer world.
Here the hardest stones warm and beat like hearts.

Old lovers find their way here,
intoxicated by the wine of hope.
Their kisses leave small glowing moons
on souls born in total darkness,
whose eyes adjust at last
to the possibilities of brilliance,
and even the dead dance
in this living light.

A Waterfall Whispers in the Night

I camp on frozen ground
where nothing grows

and no one knows
where to go from here.

A cold place of fog
that never lifts or changes,

but a safe plot
without hoot or roar,

where I feel at home but lost,
alone but haunted.

The vapor of my breath rises
with the dawn but hovers near.

A shroud of river mist
cocoons me in ghost rags,

but still a dream of light not from here
brightens a path through old trees.

Through the haze a waterfall
whispers secrets

of how ice becomes water,
becomes steam, becomes fog,

and how in a miracle of blindness
my ears can find a way.

Dualities Debate

For whatever is the matter,
there is the antimatter.

For God, a Devil in His details.

For the rose, the thorn
makes a point.

For the sake of argument,
I look on the bright side of blindness
to light my way.

Starting from the End

Where the road home dead-ends,
only the wind goes on
through the parting grass,

goes on, goes back
like the quantum minds
of children whose dreams
swing high, whose jaws
squeak with nursery rhymes,
whose yawns lullaby
into an ocean of time.

Older eyes stop at the near
horizon, do not see the sun
sail off the edge into open space.

In a possible world,
trees travel far on roots and wind.
Tied to a swaying branch,
I would go along, sail or fall
with autumn leaves.

From a distant limb ahead
a tire swing creaks,
and laughter that could be mine
is flying there.

Acknowledgments

Grateful acknowledgment to the following publications in which these poems first appeared, sometimes in earlier versions:

Amethyst Review: "A Pantheist's Hard Facts," "Obstructed View," "The Size of Infinity"
Backchannels: "Pathway"
Black Bear Review: "Condensation," "The Gentleman Who Woke Up as a Goat," "Moving to the City"
Blue Lake Review: "Everlasting Life"
Bond Street Review: "In the Living Room of the Dead"
Bookends Review: "The Flight"
The Bridge: "Lighthouse"
Burningword: "Gaia Elemental"
California Quarterly: "Discoveries of the Shovel," "The Gravedigger Blows on the Bottle"
The Cape Rock: "The Borgeyman"
Chants: "The Treasure of Bone"
The Chariton Review: "Feeding the Body of Earth"
The Chattahoochee Review: "Men"
Clarion: "Asking God to Change"
Clementine Poetry Journal: "Private Garden," "A Waterfall Whispers in the Night" (under a different title)
Construction: "Reinkarmation"
The Courtship of Winds: "The Invisible Man at the Grocery"
Dancing Shadows Review: "The Meaning of Dogs"
Dead Angel: "Why Graveyards Are Full of Bright Birds"
Dead Mule School of Southern Literature: "Fairy Tale," "Grandmother," "One Man's Profit"
Descant: "Why Buzzards Are Spoiled"
Dressing Room Poetry Journal: "Snowflakes on a Hardening Land"
East Coast Literary Review: "Voices from the Storm"
En Passant: "The Last Saint of the Empire"
ELF (Eclectic Literary Forum): "The New World Dictionary," "River Pulse"
Eunoia Review: "Where the Road Curves Back," "The Chrysalis of Coal," "Something Missing, " "Search Party"
Firefly: "Written to One of My Selves in an Alternate Universe"
The Foliate Oak Literary Magazine: "Developing a Photograph of God"
Foundling Review: "Knots," "After the War, the War"
Furtive Dalliance: "The Peace of Scenic Curtains," "Wandering Alzheimer Woods"
Gaia: A Journal of Literary & Environmental Arts: "What Missing the Cat Means," "Veterans Know a Purr Is Just an Infant Growl"
GFT Presents: One in Four: "Starting from the End"
Gnarled Oak: "When My Youth Catches Up with Me"
The Grasslands Review: "The Glass Heart"
Great River Review: "Blame It on Genealogy"
Green Hills Literary Lantern: "Progress"

Gris-Gris: "Turtles Watching the Stars"
The Habersham Review: "Regret"
Hampden-Sydney Poetry Review: "Darkness Too Is a Mirror"
Hobble Creek Review: "Charity"
Iodine Poetry Journal: "Daydreaming at Rush Hour," "How to Go Somewhere," "The Mind"
Jellyfish Whispers: "Frostline"
Kalkion: "The Last Person on Earth Goes for a Drive," "The Last Person on Earth in a Traffic Jam," "The Last Person on Earth Runs for President," "The Last Person on Earth Visits His Neighbor"
The Kenyon Review: "A Wingbeat of Hope"
The Lascaux Review: "The Dreamer Returns Home," "How to Pay Respects to a Serial Killer," "A Capitalist Back to Nature," "Putting Out the Trash"
Linden Avenue Literary Journal: "Shadow at Low Tide"
Little Dog Poetry: "Dualities Debate"
Loch Raven Review: "The Gravedigger's Pay Dirt," "Graveyard Shift," "The Gravedigger's Plot"
Lost River: "Worlds Apart"
The Lullwater Review: "Prophets Climbing to Machu Picchu"
Lungfish Review: "Why the Dead Are so Passive"
Main Street Rag: "The Wind Is Often Sudden Here," "Yellowing"
Negative Capability: "The Juggler Tells His Children of Dreams"
Neonbeam (U.K.): "Motions"
Northwind Magazine: "Hero," "Wishing Well"
Offcourse: "Blind and Barefoot," "Breakup," "Horse Trainer," "Lowering the Bucket," "70 Years Young"
OG's Speculative Fiction: "The Last Person on Earth Begins His Diary"
Pale House: "The Last Person on Earth Finds Guns Everywhere"
Pendragon: "The Ghost in the Barn Light," "The Ghost Observes His Body"
Permafrost: "Sanctuary"
Pidgeonholes: "What Goes Up"
Pinyon: "At the End of an Old Logging Road"
Pirene's Fountain: "The Landowners of Pompeii, " "Window on the Best of Impossibilities, " "Stubborn Leaf," "The Painted Forest," "The Invisible Man Works the System"
Plainsongs: "The New Dawn"
The Plastic Tower: "The Gravedigger Pacing His Cage"
Poem: "Burying a Mute," "The Death of Magic," "The Old Deeds of the Gravedigger" "Snowhaunt"
poeticdiversity: "Too Close but Light Years Apart," "The Shadows of Machu Picchu," "Homesick"
Poetry Quarterly: "Our Native Land"
Rain Dog Review: "Road Steam"
Remark Poetry: "Going Through the Motions"
Riverrun: "Dream of the Hollow Bone," "The Gravedigger's Black Apple Beating," "The Gratitude of the Dead"
The Rufous City Review: "Camping in a Late Fall Forest"
Rusty Truck: "On Mother's Day"

Serving House Journal: "Hearing an Atheist's Confession," "How to See the World"
Sheila-na-Gig: "Night Shift," "Leaving a Broken Home"
Slant: "Reshaping the Earth"
Southern Poetry Review: "Dream of the Electric Eel," "Homestead"
The Sow's Ear: "Confessions of the Slower Sprinter"
Spoon River Poetry Review: "The Light Sedative of Dark"
The Stickman Review: "Ice Steeples, Road Signs," "Rock Road," "How Trees Travel"
Still Crazy: "Passings"
Tiger's Eye Journal: "Old Storm"
Tipton Poetry Journal: "The Yellow Brick Road to Greatness," "Imposter"
Underground Voices: "The Gravedigger's Workday"
Visions International: "Against the Graveyard's Greater Wall"
Whistling Shade: "The Gravedigger's Legacy"
Wild Goose Poetry Review: "The Language of Trees, " "A Dutiful Ruler Speaks of Peace"
The Wilderness House Literary Review: "How the Invisible Go Blind"
Wildflower Muse: "Shell"
Windless Orchard: "Orphans Adopting Themselves"
Writers' Forum: "Cottonmouth Catchers in a Night Swamp"
Xanadu: "Communion," "Ice-Sparkles"

"Cleaning Up" appeared in *American Society: What Poets See* (FutureCycle Press, 2013), a Good Works project.

"The Gravedigger's Night Out" appeared in *Immortelles: Poems of Life and Death by New Southern Poets* (Xavier Review Press, 1995).

"Prescriptions for Two" appeared in *Weatherings* (FutureCycle Press, 2015), a Good Works project.

About FutureCycle Press

FutureCycle Press is dedicated to publishing lasting English-language poetry in both print-on-demand and Kindle formats. Founded in 2007 by long-time independent editor/publishers and partners Diane Kistner and Robert S. King, the press was incorporated as a nonprofit in 2012. A number of our editors are distinguished poets and writers in their own right, and we have been actively involved in the small press movement going back to the early seventies.

Each year, we have awarded the FutureCycle Poetry Book Prize and honorarium for the best original full-length volume of poetry we published that year. Introduced in 2013, our Good Works projects benefit various charities. Our Selected Poems series highlights contemporary poets with a substantial body of work to their credit; with this series we strive to resurrect work that has had limited distribution and is now out of print.

We are dedicated to giving all of the authors we publish the care their work deserves, offering a catalog of the most diverse and distinguished work possible, and paying forward any earnings to fund more great books. All of our books are kept "alive" and available unless and until an author asks that their book be taken out of print.

We've learned a few things about independent publishing over the years. We've also evolved a unique and resilient publishing model that allows us to focus mainly on vetting and preserving for posterity poetry collections of exceptional quality without becoming overwhelmed with bookkeeping and mailing, fundraising activities, or taxing editorial and production "bubbles." To find out more, come see us at futurecycle.org.

www.ingramcontent.com/pod-product-compliance
Lightning Source LLC
Chambersburg PA
CBHW060758110426
42739CB00033BA/3233